EXCELLENCE IN DRIVER TRAINING

How to be a GOOD driving instructor

Dave Foster MA, Dip.DI

Dedication

This book is dedicated to the trainers who have made me think, made me questions myself and question teaching, on how it should be done correctly. Mostly by how well they do, but a few for how badly they do. Without each and every trainer I have encountered, this book wouldn't be possible.

I would also like to dedicate this book to my driving instructors at 1st 4 Driving who like me, stride to be the best driving instructor they can be. With their determination and commitment, they too are GOOD driving instructors.

Finally, I dedicate this book to Jess, my Office Manager, who has put up with my constant requests to edit and help with inspiration for this book.

CONTENTS

how the responsibility for risk would be shar

PREFACE

In over 20 years in the driver training profession, I have met some fantastic driver trainers. I've also seen a lot who bring the profession down and this has worried me my whole career. But it is not for them I write this book. This book is written for the 'good' driving instructors. The driving instructors who strive to deliver the best driving lessons they can. The driving instructors who learn and cascade the facts and not stuff they hear from some forum. It is for the driving instructors that enjoy giving great customer service in every aspect of their role. It is also written for the many people who are not yet driving instructors but think 'I could do that' and are looking to become good driving instructors.

Driving instructors work hand in hand with the DVSA. We teach and they set the standards. The DVSA set the standards to ensure the fee-paying public get value for money from every driving lesson. They ensure that teenagers and the vulnerable are safe. We work hand in hand with the driving examiners. We do the training; they do the testing. We must keep a professional conduct and working relationship with the other professionals that make up our profession. It is a sad fact that too many driving instructors do not have this professional regard for the DVSA and examiners.

This book is written for the advancement of the profession and its standards. But above all, for the many good and often great driving instructors I see leave the profession because while they are good teachers, the business aspects often fail them. This is the reason I took a fresh look at my own Continued Professional Development as a trainer. Why I changed direction from a training company and started my own driving school. I never wanted to do this until I saw how I could help those good driving instructors continue doing what they do best while I take care of the business side.

This story started with two women working for a franchise I was Director of Training for. These girls were great (and still are) driving instructors. But they were getting almost no pupils from their franchise. Eventually I suggested they set up on their own, but they did not know how to, so I started to help. I realised there were lots like these two women who really are great instructors but do not want the business side or hassle.

This book is not just about my school, in fact there is very little in this book about that. It contains the recipe or model for any driving instructor or potential driving instructor to use as a successful business model.

Whilst I got to the top of my game in driving tuition and now in the marketing and business side, you too can do the same. This book can help prevent you from making the mistakes I made trying to find the way forward. In the early days of my driving school, we were lucky to see six phone calls a week, today we have between 100 and 200 a day. Not bad for someone who didn't want to start a driving school!

CHAPTER 1: INTRODUCTION

Who's this book for?

As an instructor trainer, I once met a trainee who all seemed good. Nice lady and good attitude, we worked through some basics then on her second session with me we worked on manoeuvres, and all was promising. Then we went onto country lanes, dual carriageways, and motorways. We hit 45mph and she would go no faster. Asking why, she explained she never has and never will go above 45mph. I was trying to coach the reasons why this might be dangerous and that she was training to be a driving instructor. I explained she would need to teach pupils safely at speeds of up to 70mph, but she was insisting that if they want to do those speeds, they will need another driving instructor. Her view was, she would teach them to 45mph, and another instructor could do the rest. She did not complete her training!! Honestly, I was looking for the camera in the car as it was so surreal. This book is not for her.

This book is for anyone thinking of becoming a **good** Driving Instructor. Note the emphasis on 'good'. This book gives the facts on not just training to become a Driving Instructor but training to be a **good** driving instructor or maybe if you are already a driving instructor and you want to know how to become a better instructor.

This may be a bold statement but, the profession is full of...

well, not very good instructors. Just take a glance at many Facebook groups, look at the tone and often, the language of driving instructors. Look at the questions they ask, questions they would berate and ridicule on Facebook if their pupils asked such questions.

Yes, I could not believe this one and the replies were often just as bad.

Or how about this one?

Really?!! These are on driving instructor forums being asked by driving instructors. I could show you many more but that's for another book one day.

For years I have seen advice from forums, books and down at the driving test centres that was, well just incorrect. Advice that often goes against that of the Highway Code and could be dangerous. Only today, I saw a question about the painted 20mph signs on the road. A driving instructor, yes, a driving instructor, was asking if they are legally enforceable. Bad enough but another instructor told him they could ignore them. Pupils ask these questions every lesson and these are great opportunities to do some coaching. For example: 'What do you think they are there for? What might happen if you ignored this advice and exceeded the limit?'.

Driving instructors have a very important role in life. They are teaching a life skill that can literally mean life. We read about young drivers being killed or seriously injured all too often. It is widely known that 1 in 5 crashes involve a young driver too. Our role is not just preparing for the driving test but to ensure the pupil has a solid and correct foundation to their future driving. Giving them every opportunity in their lessons to take responsibility when they are ready at every stage. A question from a pupil is an opportunity to turn it around into a coaching session. This helps formulate an understanding of the decisions they will need to make every day that they drive, for life. It's not an opportunity to show how clever or knowledgeable the instructor is.

There is a simple rule in life and particularly in business known as the Pareto Principle. The Pareto Principle can be transcribed as '80% of people in any industry or profession are doing it wrong'. Yep, 80% and it doesn't matter what industry or profession, the plain simple fact is 80% are wrong. Can this be true? This principle can be applied in many ways and in more detail but that's not for the purpose of this chapter.

Take a random trade, off the top of my head, electricians. Now they all seem to charge a reasonable hourly rate, they all seem busy. Everyone I've spoken to say how they are working long days and often into the weekend. Yet so many seem to be just, well, getting by. Many electricians dream of the day when they have a fleet of vans and electricians working for them. (Many also don't want this, and that is fine), while a few seem to have their dream company with vans and electricians working for them. They work in the same area, with the same customers and the same competition, so why are they doing better than the others? All will be revealed.

Within the forums and groups where learners go for

advice, they are being given wrong information, very wrong information in many cases and this can be bad for them. How do they know though? First let me give you an example of this advice and how it would look.

To signal or not

A learner asks for advice on signalling when moving off. The instructor explains 'you always signal when moving off in case there's another car who will need to see you signal'

Good advice?

Well, the learner is certainly going to think so! It sounds logical and correct, and I bet you're even thinking that too!

Well to a degree it's correct but (and isn't there always a but), it's poor or incomplete advice. Other than a learner, in certain circumstances failing a test, it could later result in a crash. (I use the term crash and not accident intentionally as an accident implies nobody was at fault).

Want to know the answer? Keep reading...

If you hadn't already guessed, this book is certainly for people who want the correct facts!

I've tried to keep the right balance of facts and important content but with a touch of humour here and there, maybe more there than here!

This book is for anyone thinking about becoming a driving instructor. The forums are full of people complaining about their training or driving school and even a few consumer rights programmes have turned their attentions to a couple of driving schools. Now this isn't always the driving schools' fault although often it is. Some people don't fully consider whether the job is right for them in the beginning. They haven't looked at a full picture of what the job entails, the training (which can be made easy by the way) or other factors such as un-realistic expectations. It's important to avoid just listening to the 'sales hype',

Yes! Some schools will give you sales hype, albeit disguised from a caring development manager or some similar title.

Do your research and get the facts and plenty of them before you decide. But don't be put off. If you read my story, you'll find out how I would not be here today if I had let the scare mongers put me off! A driving school owner once told me *'David, you'll never make a good driving instructor'. H*a, well I sit here now with a leading school, looking after many others, trained 100's and have a Master's degree in Driver Training Education. Yeah, she was right on the button, NOT! Or there's the test centre scaremongers, 'this game is finished, it used to be good but I'm off, you can have my school if you want' he's still pedalling this story 20 years on to every new driving instructor who comes his way and yes, there's one in every test centre.

I've met, rescued, and coached so many trainee driving instructors over the years and it's those people who have led me to write this book. To ensure that everyone gets the right facts. I have met many trainees that wanted to leave and give up. It was more about the other stuff that was going on than the training often. They would often reach the plateau feeling they couldn't do it. Coupled with the fact they had spent a grand of their money or in some cases a few grand of their money, they were getting scared. Then they had their partners putting on the pressure, 'when will you pass, what if you don't? etc.' Incidentally many of these instructors are still out there and some even work for me 12 years on. Am I doing something right?

It shouldn't feel like that, the process is easy, and the training can be too, after all you know how to do most of it already and I will explain in further chapters.

I've mentioned this book is also for existing driving instructors who want to know the facts. Or what I would prefer is you cascade the facts. This is a wonderful profession and there is more than enough work to go around and there always will be. Certainly, if we can raise the standard of driving tuition, not only will we see better trained drivers but greater job satisfaction. I came into this profession looking for a job. I found a vocation and in truth found myself.

So, read through the chapters, skip the ones you don't fancy if you want. While I have tried to put them in some structured order, we are all different and all have different objectives (oops going into training mode now) and we see things differently.

So, we had better look at 'why even become a driving instructor in the first place?

WHY DID I WRITE THIS BOOK?

Some years ago, I was asked a question. 'What is a franchise?' I gave this a lot of thought and looked up the dictionary meaning. 'a successful business model'. This got me thinking and I wrote a presentation for the school I was then Director of Training for. A franchise works by everyone following the same model exactly. Take McDonalds, for example (other good food outlets are available) everyone follows the same menu, the way the burger is prepared, the way the business is run, the branding. McDonalds have an enormous range of working manuals and practices each franchise MUST follow. Every good franchise is the same. But within the driver training profession, it does not seem to work that way. It has been debated long and hard whether a driving school is really a franchise and in truth it is not. However, the fact remains that many driving instructors do fail, mainly because of the business side. As a school, we turn away hundreds of pupils a week and in this post lock down period, we are turning away a hundred plus a day. The work is certainly there. So why is it that so many fail? They do not follow a successful model. The marketing of pupils is easy when you know the formulae, the website, optimisation, acquisition, selling the lessons, all of which become just a matter of routine. If we need more pupils, we do XYZ.

Delivering courses, I have often been told how much I inspire people. I remember someone saying how I should be a motivational speaker. Something else that sticks with me is someone who attended many seminars I was at, who said to me once, 'David, if anyone should write a book, it should be you.' So, after many false starts, I am back writing this book. I see far too many 'good' instructors fail. Great characters, good teachers but still fail and I know I can help them. Let's fill the test centres with good instructors and banish the rude, scruffy, couldn't care less about their pupils brigade we see every day.

Recently I have had a driving instructor leave me. Why? He has found a driving school who charge more per hour for driving lessons and less for the franchise. He is one of the best driving instructors I know with so much potential. The driving school can't be found in the front page of Google, difficult to find on social media and will probably struggle to supply pupils after the post COVID rush of pupils has ended. I am sure this instructor will end up struggling for pupils, the school will start to reduce prices to remain competitive. There is a good chance the instructor will struggle and what I normally see is they leave the profession. Disheartened, broke and their dream gone. My door is always open but pride I think stops them returning. Some do return and they stay forever but most disappear. What a shame for someone who has such potential. Please prove me wrong like I proved the trainer wrong who said I would never make it!

Facebook, oh my goodness don't get me started on Facebook! Every single day has a post about 'bin that pupil' or someone talking about 'how stupid' their pupil is or some other derogatory comment. Everyday an instructor asks something extremely basic about traffic rules. Trainees asking if they are allowed to market themselves or what the best lesson for their part three test is, where are their trainers?... Calm down David, calm down. Mind you all this went on long before Facebook, the older amongst us will remember The UK Driving Instructors Forum. Who remembers my old mate 'Airmiles' as he was known? I can't reveal his real identity, but he certainly challenged many an instructor who showed ill slip shod ways.

The guy knew what he was talking about, he attended more CPD than many and not just in this country. He regularly attends the Driving Instructor conferences in America too and I'm sure he went to Dubai for the world conference.

So, in this book, I share mine and many others 'successful business model', so that you too can be successful. Whether you are thinking about becoming a driving instructor or are already an instructor, then you will get something from this book. I don't expect everyone to agree with everything, and that's their choice but it IS a successful model and there's nothing difficult about it.

WHO AM I TO WRITE THIS BOOK?

This chapter is not written to boast, well maybe a little bit. I am very proud of my achievements for very personal reasons. You see I came from a very ordinary background with parents choosing to draw benefits rather than work. (I use the word 'choosing' correctly) Living on a council estate, that the council paid my parents money to move to. My parents were not supportive, far from it. I was told many times, 'David will never amount to much'. My school education was below average. School saw me playing the fool most of the time and skiving. The only reason I liked school was because I wasn't at home. My grades were poor however my escape was my brief career in the Royal Navy to which incidentally I passed my entrance exams with very high marks. One thing I could do naturally is mend things. It didn't matter what, give me a box of pieces, and I would work out how to re-assemble. Give me a broken TV, and I would find out how to fix it. (Before the days of the internet). So naturally I spent my career mending things. First, cars, then I took my City and Guilds qualifications in electronics and started repairing tv and video then later automatic control systems for doors. When taking my City and Guilds, I was one of the few to pass the control systems element with a distinction. Was something emerging? So, a normal, non-academic background.

MY TRAINING BIT.

I first had the idea to become a driving instructor back in 1991. However, I thought the fees then of £1800 too expensive so shelved it. In 1998 finding myself redundant, looked at it again. The fees were still roughly the same and I looked around a few driving schools. It was a difficult decision and one I foolishly made on finances only, I went for the cheapest!! I set up an instalment plan with them paying over 6 months. A week later and a box of books arrived, when I say box, crate is more of a description as it must have measured 3 feet square. I set about studying for the part one driving instructor's theory test. This was not difficult and 2 months later I had passed the part one first time. And so on to the part two practical driving test. I had about 5 lessons each 2 hours long where various 'bad habits' were pointed out but the odd bit for me was missing out gears and block gear changing. A strange concept at first but one I now appreciate. The other odd thing was not signalling every time I moved off, I was told (and I now completely understand this principle) to make sure you take good, effective observation and if there is nobody there, who are you signalling to? Err yes, it makes sense. If there was somebody coming, would I move off? Err no, so again no signal. In fact, if you signal out of habit, as many of us do and there was a road opposite, we could fail a driving test for misleading signals. Now remember I mentioned this in an earlier chapter. A couple of months later I was sitting holding my first-time pass for my part two driving test.

And now the fun began. I was still with the same instructor who gave excellent part two driving tuition. But part three, the ability to instruct, was different. I basically got in the car with him, and I was told 'deliver a driving lesson on moving off and stopping'. No tuition, no guidance, no instruction. Guess what? I was rubbish, or so I thought. As I tried to control this trainer who role played a young 17-year-old (yes, I know not good role play now) he drove up pavements, stalled, put it in the wrong gear, started the engine in gear, twisted his seat belt, left the door open and a whole host more faults. Never in all my years by the way has an instructor seen a pupil display all these faults at once so don't be put off. Now I KNOW, his role play was bad, very bad and it did nothing for my self-esteem or confidence. I thought all pupils would be like this. I thought I am rubbish and can't teach him or control him. And now for the best bit, after being told by him all my faults and about my lack of teaching, he then explained 'next week we move on to the next stage, junctions. Umm so I can't teach you to move off but next week we'll try junctions. Well rinse and repeat, next week I was equally rubbish and he told me so and then we moved on to crossroads and so on. I was believing I could not do this and took a break in my training.

Now earlier you may remember I told you about an 'expert' who told me 'David I believe in telling the facts even if you won't like what I am saying but David you will never make a driving instructor'. Yes, it's time for her.

I went to another school; the owner told me she was an expert and had trained people that other schools could not train. Well, she plonked me in a car with her son as a pupil and told me basically 'he's not very good with mirrors, some other stuff and to teach him'. Still, I have had no actual training in how to do this, how to even identify a fault let alone analyse it and remedy it. As a result, I was even more confident I could NOT do this. I took a job in a factory and practically gave up. Then one day I thought, as I hated the factory, I would give it one more try. I contacted the original driving school and asked if they had another trainer, and I was introduced to Dave

Sweatman. Now I try to keep my source confidential, but this man deserves every credit due to him because if it wasn't for him, I would not be here now. This man in one session restored my faith in myself. First, he asked my background and after I explained how I could fix anything he said, 'well this will be easy then because you'll be fixing driving'. And so, it was, I was shown how to apply what I already knew to my new role and so it began. I identified a fault, I analysed the cause, I made a remedy and ensured the fault would not return. Dave was using coaching although I'm not sure he realised it at the time. And I passed my part three first time with a 5-5 which was a very good grade.

The above story I tell you, so you know that you too can do this. During training, almost all trainees hit this plateau where they think they can't do it. Many give up. I find that I spend a lot of my time convincing trainees they can do it and I am so glad I have. As I said before, some of these trainees now work for me still, 15 years on. I believe anyone can be trained, in fact I now say anyone can learn any subject they want, whoever they are even if it is or was their worst subject.

So, life as a driving instructor began, but why am I qualified to write with authority, why listen to me? Well, I've been here now for over 20 years, I took my qualification and thought I can do more. The concept of teaching got to me, and I thought, I know I can do better. So, I enrolled in what was then the Driving Instructors Association (DIA) Diploma in Driving Instruction (Dip.DI). Now remember my background, and I hated writing so being told I had to write 5 written papers on different subjects was scary but to cut a long story short I did it, and in 2 years. In fact, I later became a question writer and examiner for the same qualification.

THE ACADEMIC BIT

Wanting to know more about the teaching side, I enrolled in an adult education course that led to a Certificate in Education (Cert.Ed.). I attended every seminar and conference I could and was co-opted onto the DIA's General Purposes Committee (GPC). I later became their chairman although I couldn't quite follow my predecessor Don McQuillen-Wright, a legend in his own bow tie. He was another very professional and influential man to me. After fleet qualifications, ORDIT and many other things I enrolled into Middlesex University to do my BA (Hons) degree and later my master's degree that again I passed with a distinction. This degree was specifically on the training of driving instructors and put together all my work in this field. It was considered unique and innovative and has been my work since. Later I attended Dr Jonathon Passmores course at The University of East London on Coaching and the Qualified Driver. There have been many more course and seminars but suffice to say I am still learning like we all are or should be. I have done this so I can cascade this out to other instructors so they can help teach better and safer drivers. I believe the profession needs new, better qualified instructors who will move the profession on.

I want to inspire you more; let you know that you can get through the hard times. I write many articles and one day in one of my articles I quoted a saying from Socrates about how anyone can learn anything with the right motivation. Someone challenged me and asked if I really believed that. I thought about it and questioned myself. I was asked 'what was my worst subject in school?'. An easy choice, I hated English grammar, didn't understand it, and never wanted to. So, the challenge was set for me to learn English grammar, whoopee! I looked at how I could do this and decided to not only learn it, but to try to be able to teach it. Suffice to say, six months later I was a qualified teacher of Teaching English as foreign language (TEFL). More so, I love English grammar now and as I am currently learning to speak Spanish (yes, I never stop learning) it has been a great help.

And so, the story continues, but today you are more likely to find me studying marketing because without pupils, you can't earn and if you can't earn you can't train better, safer drivers and put food on your table. So just like my master's degree, I am, and quite successfully looking at marketing now. Most of our areas are now top of Google, we turn pupils away every day and that's not good. You don't have to do what I did, partly why I did it, so you don't have to, but I am certainly the person to get you there.

I promise the rest of this book is now about you!

So, we know it's for me, is it for you?

IS IT REALLY FOR YOU?

Being a driving instructor and working your own hours, being your own boss, seems like the ideal job. But in a way you have lots of bosses, your pupils, and their parents. You need a lot of self-discipline to turn up for work when the sun is shining. I see novice instructors all too easily fall for the pressures of 'let's go to the beach today' or 'the demands from the partner to go shopping etc.' It often seems too easy to just send a text and cancel those lessons. I see it a lot. It starts with one day, then two then a week. Then we get the complaints in the office about unreliability.

Recently we had a qualified instructor join us. We started to get phone calls from their pupils about not turning up. We tried to contact the instructor to find out why. We could only leave messages. Three days later, and more not turning up for pupils, we get a message saying their daughter had a baby and was so ill they needed their support. Ok, this happens. Then two weeks later it all starts again and this time we see a post on Facebook about how pupils are being unreasonable because she has had to take time off because the daughter has had a baby that night. Hold on we are thinking, same daughter who had one 2 weeks ago or another one? Two weeks later it starts again this time their father was ill. Meanwhile we keep seeing posts on Facebook of them at the beach, out for meals and partying. Pupils were rightly complaining because they were not being told. One pupil was driven by their parents some distance to a pre-arranged meeting point to find the instructor has not turned up and can't get hold of them.

The above instructor is no longer with us, but we still see post from that instructor about how unreasonable her pupils are because of this and that reason. Now these sorts of things happen, take one of our instructors who get told in the night their mother had sadly passed away. They make one phone call to us; we tell the instructor we'll deal with the pupils, and they just go sort things out with the family. We contact all the pupils, and they are fine and understand this. We keep the pupils informed and everyone is happy.

When pupils pass their tests, it's great but we all get a run where they don't. You need to be able to pick yourself up and look to see IF there is anything you can do. I've helped many with sudden runs of test fails, some who have been teaching for 15 plus years.

Looking smart and keeping the car smart goes without saying but keeping this up is not easy. It is all too easy to just think 'what the heck' and not bother to change from the gym clothes or gardening clothes or whatever. Planning that time to get into the teaching zone or frame of mind. And if you get a gap in lessons, what do you do? Initially I found it all too easy to just pop home but that made it worse coming out to work again. So eventually I did not come home between lessons but went to a local supermarket car park and did some study or diary work, cleaned the car, or just treated myself to a breakfast or something. To me, I was at work from 8am to 6pm. This really helped.

Great patience is needed, but it's more than that. Some instructors complain because pupils cancel lessons all the time. I have written a lot on this, and the reason is not because of a lesson break, no money, or need to concentrate on other studies, these are just the excuses the pupils give. The simple fact is, they don't want to be in the car with that instructor. For one reason or another, they will make excuses. We see this occasionally where an instructor will keep losing pupils. I did research on this years ago. The pupils were saying they changed instructors because, their instructor shouted, was smelly, always late for lessons or did not make them feel comfortable. Their instructors were giving the other reasons of lesson breaks, no money, studies, etc. One instructor had received 117 pupils in 10 months and had an empty diary, working for the same school an instructor in the same postcode with a full diary had received 23 pupils and had closed his diary. That's also 117 pupils saying the school and driving instructor are rubbish to school friends and family... eek. A good franchise can help with this and support you with good customer and business skills.

Some of your pupils will be a breath of fresh air, some will seem like the spawn of the devil. Being able to teach both is a skill. Fortunately, it's a skill you can learn. I've worked a lot of speed awareness courses and the ones I enjoyed the most were when someone challenged me. When someone says, 'the cameras are just about making money aren't they!' I like the challenge and can easily coach them to a different view. At first it was not easy but soon it becomes habit, today I just think 'that old chestnut' and go into coaching mode. The same is with pupils, 'My dad says he only took 6 lessons' ah that old chestnut or 'My mum says I don't need to learn about the turn in the road' ah that old chestnut. All can be coached and easily sorted but without getting confrontational. Please! Don't get confrontational, it's a slippery road to failing.

Put money aside for a rainy day or something. It's easy to just spend all the money but as I mentioned before, put it all into a separate account and pay a wage. It also becomes so much easier with the accounts at the end of the year.

Being professional in everything you do, whether it's posting on social media, at the shops or in the car teaching. Dress, act and behave as your pupils or probably more importantly, your pupils' parents would want to see. If you have or had a 17-year-old child, how would you want their instructor to be? Look on social media and see how many forget this fact. You are always in the public eye.

Create habits, a friend and author of The Routine Machine (Lamerton, 2019), John Lamerton talks about those habit-forming routines that turn 'consistency into a superpower' (thanks John for this quote). Habits are good, make a specific time to do the accounts, make time to eat breakfast, form a habit to plan each lesson, cancelled lesson? Wash the car. This book is being written from a habit. I write early in the morning and when I've hit over 1000 words, the rest is a bonus and I get a coffee. (My reward LOL).

I was training someone to be an instructor. Let's call him Martin (not real name). Martin was an ex-drill instructor for the army. Suddenly, Martin hit me when I made a mistake whilst I was role playing a pupil. Not a hard hit, more of a tap but was a hit all the same. I talked about how he could not do this with his pupils although at first, he could not see why not, it was only a tap. I explained about never making contact and the invisible wall between instructor and pupil. He seemed to get the message. While out on a subsequent training session with another trainee in the back, I again role playing made a fault and he produced a very sharp pencil and stabbed me with it. Again, just a poke but he explained you said *I was not allowed* to touch the *pupil; I did not touch you!* and he had not touched me! Much explaining later he still felt it was not fair but accepted it. He was always in my books as the instructor to read about later as, *the* most likely *instructor* to appear in a newspaper, as he passed his part three and became a driving instructor. The instructor sat in the rear, still works for me today and we often re-tell the story of Martin The pencil Collins. (Not real name.)

CHAPTER 2: BECOMING A 'GOOD' DRIVING INSTRUCTOR.

Why become a driving instructor

I'm sitting here drafting this chapter and trying not to make it a sales letter. But it's difficult because to me, there are so many good reasons to become a good driving instructor. So, I suddenly thought I would include a following chapter on 'why not become a driving instructor' to address the balance. So, with that in mind I will explain the benefits and reasons why to become a good driving instructor.

XYZ School of motoring
URGENTLY REQUIRE
Driving instructors
• TRAIN TO BECOME A DRIVING INSTRUCTOR
• EARN £40,000 PLUS A YEAR
• WORK THE HOURS YOU WANT
• DRIVE A BRAND-NEW CAR

The adverts reads,

Can this be true? Well yes it can be, it must be to be able to be advertised. But the devil is in the detail.

WHAT YOU CAN EARN

Yes, you can earn more than £40,000 per year (today, you are more likely to earn more than £40,000 or even £50,000) but read my chapter on 'will I really earn £40,000+' later. With a Driving School franchise, you generally keep all the lesson fees. There are a few that have a different arrangement. So, some simple maths can tell you what you can earn. Assume a lesson fee of £35 per hour and you want to do a 40-hour week. This would work out as £67,200 a year (taking 4 weeks holiday a year). Minus cost of Franchise £4250, car lease/purchase probably similar and fuel £2880 then net is still £55,770 There will be insurance and other small costs, but you can see it's achievable. Driving lessons with my Driving School are currently £36 an hour. You do the maths on this one.

Franchise fees can differ widely. The big schools tending to charge the highest, to some local schools who are basically farming out their spare work. In the middle are the local/regional driving schools often working hard to provide marketing and support similar if not better than the big driving schools sometimes. Independent driving instructors do not pay a franchise fee however, they must do their own marketing, answer the phone and many other jobs. For the record, in business 'word of mouth' is not considered marketing. Marketing is something you have control over and can turn on and off. You need many different avenues to marketing as if anyone of them fail, you're left with nothing coming in. More on this later

WORKING HOURS

One of the greatest benefits of the job is being able to work the hours you want. I decided quite early on that I didn't want to work weekends. I think it was after a brief career as an ice cream salesperson, going round estates with my chimes on watching all those people in their windows eating their Sunday roasts.

You can certainly fit the role around the school hours, hobbies, or any other commitment but you will need to identify, or your driving school will need to identify your 'target market' that would want driving lessons during YOUR working hours. We call target markets **avatars,** and I can tell you many driving schools will have no idea what 'avatars' are and will think it's just the name of some movie!!

DRIVE A BRAND-NEW CAR.

The larger driving schools tend to supply the car. These cars are leased to the driving school on very favourable terms. It was once reported that one of the largest driving schools actually paid nothing for the cars that were replaced every 6 months. However, these schools tend to be the most expensive too. Smaller firms that supply the car can sometimes own them, but they often tend to be more basic models and are often kept longer. Most driving schools will lease the vehicles or help you to lease the vehicle from one of the specialists driving school lease companies. There are many advantages to this because the vehicle does not come with the school. Leasing through one of these companies is very easy and only requires a basic credit check to be done. Even driving instructors or potential driving instructors can lease with a poor credit history. If you did need to move school or decided to go independent, the car is effectively yours. You can of course with some schools, use your existing car if suitable or purchase one. With leasing yourself or purchasing, you get a greater choice of the car you want. A few driving schools do specify the car and even the colour. I like to have a variety of cars because occasionally (very occasionally) a pupil likes to ask for a specific car or even colour would you believe.

JOB SATISFACTION

Well, I must put this down with a big yes because of the huge amount of job satisfaction I get from this career. From the moment I took out my first learner, the first driving test I ever did, the first instructor trainer who passed with me to even writing these words now, all give me so much satisfaction. I often, while giving talks to driving instructors ask them 'what does it feel like when your pupil passes their driving test' and it's always met with a fantastic response. If you want it, and you enjoy the job it can be fantastic. You are helping people to do something they have been dreaming of for many years. I am doing this with these words even. I truly want YOU and people like you to find what I found in this great profession.

I truly want YOU and people like you to find what I found in this great profession.

You become a sought after and valuable member of your community making lots of new friends. Everyone remembers their driving instructor, some for good reasons and some for not so good. Taking learners from novice to test standard and beyond is great. Often, they will struggle but in time you will recognise these struggles and you will be able to fill them with confidence knowing that these are temporary blips in their learning. Like one of my more mature pupils, who thought she would never make it. Many times, she asked me why I bothered with her when she threw up another problem. She abandoned the car twice on a roundabout, fortunately she was not built for speed, and I was able to catch up with her. She passed her driving test on her third attempt. I met this very same pupil some years later in another town where she had just driven 25 miles with her friends too. They were shopping and this lady came over to me and introduced me as the man who made their shopping trip possible. Yes, I felt very proud because I knew the work that we BOTH put in.

Unlike my schoolteacher friends, your pupils want to sit in your lessons. (Most of them anyway) They sit waiting for you to arrive and are genuinely sad when the driving lessons end.

PROSPECTS

There are many avenues to explore here. I initially became a **fleet corporate trainer**. This took me out to companies where I would assess and correct any driving problems where needed. It's totally different work and extremely interesting. One day you might be with the cleaner, the next the managing director. There is a growing need for this type of work due to health and safety and the driving for work directive issued from the government.

I later went into **driving instructor training** where I later specialised and became a leading authority in training. (See later chapter) Instructor training allows you to teach not only the driving aspects but the teaching side. Teaching or rather coaching people from all walks of life. Then later seeing them teach learners or in my case, see them grow their own driving schools.

I spent quite a few years delivering **classroom training** on behalf of the police to drivers on the rehabilitation of offender's scheme. That's a big name for people caught speeding or on their phones while driving for example. This was immensely interesting work and a role I enjoyed very much. If I made even one small difference, then I knew my job was done. While on almost every course, 24 unhappy people would turn up, 22 of them left shaking my hand saying, they 'enjoyed it, and it will make a difference'. Let's not talk about the other 2 eh!

There are many more opportunities out there, companies sometimes higher in-house trainers. I know people who have gone on to work in health and safety and there are many opportunities abroad in places like Saudi Arabia, and Oman for example.

Opportunities are there IF you want them, but many driving instructors just look at the opportunity to keep becoming better at teaching the learner. Improving their teaching and service they offer. I think the trick is to keep getting better at whatever it is you do. This gives a lot of satisfaction on its own.

I used to find I got a lot of enquiries from the hard of hearing. I ended up doing a lot of work for the Royal School for the Deaf in Exeter. One day I received an email from someone saying how they were 'profoundly deaf' and if I could meet for a chat about teaching him to drive. I met them in a café in Exeter, and he was indeed profoundly deaf and had recently had cochlear implants fitted, something he was struggling with for a while. We agreed to use a communicator system that he had where I wore a transmitter around my neck, and he plugged the receiver into his implant. He told me to keep the transmitter in the car for lessons as he had lots of them. On a lesson after his, my phone that would simply make a small beep for a message kept going off every few seconds. My family are told that if they need me, keep calling and it will alert me. I got my pupil to pull over and turn off the engine, apologised for the interruption, and looked at the 30+ messages from this previous deaf pupil. Apparently, I had forgotten to turn the communicator off. It had such a good range it was still picking up my conversation with the next pupil and he was in a meeting and kept hearing our conversation as we drove past. Oops!

With this same profoundly deaf chap, he was initially struggling with some of the routines but on one lesson it all seemed to click, and his driving was so much improved. We used to have many conversations after in the café and I told him how pleased I was with his progress. He explained how he had a fantastic driving instructor. I can tell you it almost brought a tear to my eye until he let me down with the joke 'and he's cheaper than you'. Yes, he had a fantastic sense of humour, but then he needed to as his job was one of the governors at Exeter prison. I got a huge amount of job satisfaction with teaching anything out of the ordinary.

WHY NOT TO BECOME A DRIVING INSTRUCTOR

So, why NOT become a driving instructor? I put this chapter in to give a balanced view. Teaching people to drive is not for everybody. There have been a very small number of people who literally hated it. Sitting in the car scared to death. It's extremely rare for an instructor to have a crash with a pupil and if they do, it's a low-speed rear end shunt. Most driving school cars are crashed while being driven by the driving instructor themselves while not giving tuition. Although there is a growing trend for driving school cars to be used by other members of the family, like their teenage children to go out for the evening, and they are being crashed then. I have never quite understood why some instructors allow others to use the vehicle, a tool for their business, out to anyone like their children. Workers are normally very protective about their tools. If they lend them out and need to use them, there are problems. If they come back broken, problems. The driving school car is a tool and an important one. If you get a problem, you might not be able to work and could lose money. Protect your tools at all costs. Maybe because of my service engineer background I see it like this, but I think it is good advice.

Generally, as driving instructors you are very safe, and you are shown how to avoid getting into 'scrapes' during training. (Some trainers will anyway)

You are most likely to be self-employed. Although the facts about this are covered later, it's worth mentioning some stuff here. With a salaried position, each week or month you draw a salary equal to one week or month of your yearly salary. Driving lessons seem to have their peaks and troughs. There are busy weeks and quieter weeks. For example, Christmas is usually dead and the first few weeks of the summer holidays. This is when I tended to take my holidays, so it did not matter to me. In the early days, you can get a bit worried about 'will the money come in' or 'will there be enough pupils.' If you are the sort of person who might worry about these things, one way to help with this is, stay with a good franchise who will supply the work. Pupils will always need driving lessons and there are ways to deal with the troughs. Looking at your diary early to see what potential driving tests are coming up and allowing the school to fill spaces early. I know instructors who run their diaries down, panic and scream for pupils. Some, as one pupil passes, ask for another. With my school, I am usually able to do this quickly but some of the nationals, who are feeding many instructors I hear from the forums struggle with this.

It can seem the money can be up and down, but if you put all your lesson fees into a separate bank account and pay yourself a wage, it levels out just like an employed position. This takes discipline and routine but if you think you would worry, then this is the best way.

Whilst all adverts say something like 'earn £40,000 plus and work the hours you want' if you only want to work 10 hours a week, you will not earn £40,000. Likewise, if you restrict your working area to the road you live in, you or your driving school will struggle to find you work. You should not have to work too big an area but occasionally if you need work, it's wise to open your postcodes a little. For my instructors I suggest starting off with a larger (not too large) area and cut back as the diary fills up.

The income is directly related to the hours you work. I had one instructor who told us he only wanted to work in one postcode area where he lived. This area was typically lived in by retired people in their bungalows. He refused to travel to the next area, 15 minutes away. We struggled to get work in his specific postcode but were turning away lots in the next area. It really was a shame. He left us saying we were rubbish because we could not get any in his specific very small postcode area.

TYPES OF DRIVING SCHOOLS

THE NATIONAL

Driving Schools differ in their set up and ways they operate. The larger schools will tend to have directors or larger companies owning them where shareholders receive income. They have staff running them and often lots of staff. Their running costs are therefore higher and hence franchise fees are higher. But they do have the budgets to advertise greater and often. They often run discounted vouchers for students and no further cost to you. They have specialist staff who can help with issues and a huge customer service department recruiting, answering the phones, and dealing with all the business side. I think nearly all these schools have gone into or come close to going into administration at some point although most are still surviving.

THE REGIONAL

There are smaller local or regional schools who are normally run by driving instructors or ex-driving instructors where they have grown from their own school. They have maybe a few staff answering the phone or use an outside call answering service. They understand the local market and hopefully have a few avenues of marketing and not just one. They can be a bit hit and miss around the support you will receive, and pupil supply can sometimes be erratic with some. I have seen a few close recently or where the owner has gone back to his own single car school. But there are some very good ones out there.

THE ONE-MAN BAND

There are some smaller schools who maybe take on an instructor to basically do the overspill of work they can't handle. There is no real marketing plan and if work dries up, guess who's not getting any pupils? Some just sell on pupils at a fee, pupils who have asked for them, but the instructor can't currently accommodate them, so they sell them on. This is not always a good thing as pupils might be disappointed, they could not have their recommended instructor. It's not really a way to grow a school, rather a way for the instructor to make a few extra quid.

THE INTENSIVE SCHOOL

There are a few intensive driving schools out there selling a complete course. They will often take the money from a pupil, sell them the course including dates and test times and then try to find and instructor to cover. Any instructor to cover! Usually at short notice so often using unreliable instructors. I have worked with 2 such schools and never have I seen so many complaints with driving schools as with this practice. The driving schools often struggle to meet the demands of the pupil's test by not finding an instructor to cover and end up having to refund the pupil leaving to a lot of unhappy pupils. I am sure there are some out there that operate this system and it works but I have yet to find them. One school would try hard never to return the pupils money saying it was non-refundable, they were a nightmare.

THINK CAREFULLY ABOUT YOUR ROUTE BECOMING A DRIVING INSTRUCTOR!

Being a driving instructor can be, no, IS a great profession but I'm sure people have ended up disillusioned by the profession because of joining the wrong franchise or going independent and finding trying to market for pupils, answer the phone and deliver driving lessons is too much. They end up leaving the profession. I certainly could not do the marketing AND be a full-time instructor. I know how much work is involved. Today, I am a full-time marketer, and I have staff to help, with my driving school although I do the occasional teaching session for instructor trainees.

If you find a bad franchise, don't tar them all with the same brush but try again. If you go independent and find it's too much hard work, then go find a good franchise, they do exist. I'd like to think I am there for my instructors. Not just for the work stuff but over the years I'd like to think I've helped the instructors that have come to me with the many diverse personal issues such as debt, health, relationships, court appearances, and many other things.

Think carefully but please don't be put off, the money is great, and the benefits are great too!

For many years, I have looked after a few other driving schools. Call answering, business advice, payments etc. We had a lady call one of these driving schools and book in a driving lesson for her daughter's 17th birthday, six months in advance. We made the booking on behalf of the school and placed it into one of the instructors' diaries. Each month before, the mother would call checking it was all on for the big day as they were preparing a big surprise. Apparently, the daughter had gone through a lot with the loss of her father and believed she would not be able to afford driving lessons. The month for the lessons came and mum kept calling and we would check with the school owner everything was OK. Yes, we are told. The day before mum checked with us, we checked the diary and with the school owner and everything fine. Then 15 minutes after the lesson is due to start, mum calls, 'where is the instructor?' We call the school owner, who eventually gets hold of the instructor who is out shopping. He, we find out later, never looks in his diary. The mum is calling back every minute and is hysterical, I mean screaming and shouting how we have ruined her daughter's life. We explained our position as third party, but she was not happy. I could not blame her; six months this had been in the diary and just shocking service. The trouble was there was nothing that could be done at this point to ever remedy this situation. Meticulous planning and let down by a simple lack of professionalism. This could so simply have been avoided, you decide who by.

DRIVING
INSTRUCTORS
STORIES

NATALIE

Natalie had finished a foundation degree in tourism and had two jobs, delivering car parts, and working at her local Tesco. Living in deepest Cornwall there was not a huge amount of opportunity, but she had always liked driving and thought she would make a good teacher. Natalie first came to me while I was an employed instructor trainer for a large national training school. In fact, as she approached the car for the first time, I thought she was a potential learner about to ask how much my driving lessons were. Trying to not make eye contact as I was hoping not to have to explain, I only do instructor training. However, she came right up to my window and asked if I was Dave and introduced herself as my trainee. She looked almost too young. Natalie took to training very well. She used her time delivering car spares to help and practice properly her driving and soon passed her part two test. Then we moved on to part three and again this flowed well. I had no problem recommending her for a trainee licence to a driving school operating in her area. Shortly after this I was taken on by the same driving school as their director of training. This meant I was able to continue Natalie's, and many others training. Natalie passed part three. After about two years with this school, it became apparent that they were not providing pupils and services for her or many others. I talk about this in other chapters, so I helped Natalie and another driving instructor in a similar position to set up their own school that later I took on board as my own school for better services. Natalie now trains driving instructors for me and has not looked back. Because of a back condition, she sometimes needs flexible hours and being a driving instructor for a school gives her this.

TONY

Tony had spent most of his former life in the transport industry. He came to driving instruction through a large national training school but was not getting the training he needed. Like many I met Tony on a rescue course that he attended with me. My simple approach helped Tony and many others see where they had gone wrong and how to pass the part three. Later I helped Tony set up his own driving school however due to health reasons and the stress of running his own school, Tony left the industry. Tony had problems with a trainee instructor and an ADI who was getting very bad reviews for the driving school. Upon a discussion with Tony, it was agreed I'd take over the driving school. Sometime later, I was delighted when Tony called me and asked if he could work for me on a franchise. This worked well for Tony without the stress and hassle. If Tony needed pupils, he called and got them. If he needed support or advice, he would call, and we would have a chat. Tony later became a coach for me and has only recently retired.

VINCE

Vince worked previously in the pub trade, but the long hours were taking their toll on him. Like Tony, Vince came to me on a rescue course having had poor training from a large national school. He was lost, like so many others and just did not think he could pass. My simple approach helped him see the light and he passed on his next attempt. Today Vince has his own driving school that associates with my driving school. He attends every training session I ever offer and ensures trainees that work for him do too. Strangely Vince works long hours but enjoys his work now. He does take holiday now though where he can be found in his static caravan in North Devon, his favourite place.

WILL I REALLY HAVE ENOUGH WORK?

This has got to be many peoples biggest fear. In theory, yes of course you will. There will always be enough work for GOOD instructors. However, if you become one of the pupil hungry instructors always losing pupils, then no, or at least it will be difficult. There is also a simple fact told to me first by the Driving Instructors Association and then the DVSA. That 4 out of 5 driving instructors go bust within 2 years of trading. Now my own research has shown that these are the pupil hungry ones or those that just do not offer the professional customer service. There seems to be a trend. A driving instructor joins a franchise, has enough pupils, and thinks they can go independent. Two years on the recommendations dry up and so does the pupil supply and they leave the profession saying how the industry is rubbish. All the time a good franchise is turning away lots of pupils.

I remember 2 very prominent and vocal instructors telling everyone on a social media site, to go independent they have never had it so good. All you need do; they would say is set up a Facebook page. One is now a bus driver and the other a delivery driver for a supermarket.

There are many independent instructors who have been there for many years and will continue to do so but like any business you will have pupils IF you market correctly, or you let someone market for you. As I write this, it's post COVID and as a school we are turning away over 400 pupils a week. Pre-COVID it was 100 a week. Every Tom, Dick and Bad driving instructor is busy. But this won't last. It will drop down to pre-COVID levels again and the bad instructors will struggle.

If you are like me, at 17 you could not wait to get your driving licence. The same if more so is true today. Nothing will get in the way of people wanting to learn to drive. However back then, many took around 10 hours of driving lessons. Today the DVSA say the average is over 45 hours of professional tuition plus 22 hours of private practice. While the number of learners has dropped over the last 40 years by maybe 20% (due to birth rates), the number of lessons is up by 400%. Each learner is going to give you on average over £1000. How many do you need? Then there's the growing fleet market, that's working with qualified drivers in companies or qualified drivers who want refresher lessons for one reason or another. Plus, disability is often no longer a barrier to learning to drive.

WILL I REALLY EARN £40,000+

Ever since I have been in the profession, the figure £40,000 plus has been used as an advert to join the profession. It has been criticised many times by people on social media as unrealistic. Yet, many out there have been achieving this figure for a long time. In fact, the figure is out of date and should read £50,000 plus. Let's look at why.

CASE STUDY
MICHAEL

Michaels lesson rate is £33 an hour or £310 for a block of 10 hours. Michael does a mix of both hourly and block lessons, so his average hourly rate is £32, and he does 36 teaching hours a week. So, Michael receives £1152 a week in lesson payments.

Michael pays £70 a week franchise, £75 a week car lease, £65 a week on fuel, Leaving Michael £942 a week. There are a few other miscellaneous items around £15 a week. Yearly this is around £45,000 income after franchise and car costs. Assuming a 4-week holiday too!

CASE STUDY LYN:

Lyn's lesson rate is £36 an hour and £350 for a block of 10 hours. With an average lesson rate of £36 an hour. Lyn does just 26 teaching hours a week, so Lyn receives £936 a week in payments.

Lyn owns her car but has a small loan of £35 a week and franchise of £90 a week, fuel is £60. So, after these costs Lyn's makes £751 a week with around £10 in additional costs. Lyn takes 6 weeks off a year earning £34,546.

Everyone's deductions will be different, depending on if you lease, buy, or own your vehicle. Franchise payments can be different. If you don't franchise then you could deduct those costs, but you're then left with your own marketing costs, website, lead generation and a lot more admin. This suits some people.

How many pupils do you need for this? All our pupils take 2-hour lessons so 18 a week, yes just 18 a week. I used to do 3 pupils Monday and Friday and 4 pupils on Tuesday, Wednesday, and Thursday. Giving me a late start of Monday and early finish on Friday. I also used to do occasional Saturdays for something called Pass Plus. This was a 6-hour lesson with one pupil post-test on Motorways and things. There were discounted insurance advantages for the pupil, and they were very popular.

As a franchised school, I do everything possible to ensure all my instructors have the work they need. Hand on heart, not one of my instructors is needing any more work than we give them. We are turning away many pupils. I used to be director of training of a medium sized franchise and almost all their instructors were screaming for work all the time. It was one of the reasons I left. Too many sad stories of good instructors going bust because their franchise did not provide for them.

SUMMARY

I could never understand at first why, some instructors complained about the achievable £40,000. Over 20 years in and I know exactly why. I can't name the highly qualified professional who said this to me once, but he said on this subject, 'many driving instructors would be unemployable in any other walk of life'. I know exactly what he meant! It comes down to being a good instructor again, if you are, you will do well. It's something I teach you to become, and I have written a guide on it that all **DTE-Elite** and **1st 4 Driving** instructors receive. Some don't bother to read it, guess what happens to them usually!

One day, I was answering the phones when I took a call from a lad. I went through the usual postcode, provisional licence and any experience bit. He had a theory pass and told me he had never driven a car before. I start to ask about his availability when he says he needs one lesson this morning at 11am then another at 2.30 this afternoon. I start to explain how we could not fill a lesson that quickly when he says, 'it has to be today, I have my driving test this afternoon and I don't have a car'. A quick look around the office and I can see any cameras from 'Beadles about'. I ask again if he has ever driven before and he insists not but he has played a lot of video games and 'how hard can it be, it isn't rocket science'. No, he did not get a lesson with us that day!

There will always be work for good instructors, if you market well or get someone to market for you. I chose to stop working for my own school in the early days and join a franchise. Not because I did not have enough pupils, but I wanted to concentrate on being the best instructor I could. I went out and got additional qualifications while the franchise did my marketing. It's odd how I've come full circle and today all the training courses and books I read are about marketing and business.

IS SELF-EMPLOYED WORTH IT?

Separate business from personal, I mentioned before about putting your lesson fees into a separate account and drawing a weekly/monthly wage but separating business from personal is more than just that. I run a limited company. With a limited company, the company has in law its own identity. Even being self-employed it's worth thinking of your business, car, money etc. as separate from your personal life and treating your business like a tool. Your car is a tool for business with personal use added on. It's not a personal car you use for business. I mentioned before how driving instructors quite happily lend their cars to newly qualified teenage children to go out for the evening etc. If the vehicle is damaged, they can't work or earn money. This act has caused driving instructor insurance premiums to rise over recent years...

DO DRIVING SCHOOLS SUPPLY THE CAR?

Some do and some don't. Some say they do and, they lease them and pass the cost to you. Let's look at the options.

DRIVING SCHOOL SUPPLIES CAR AND FRANCHISE AS ONE PACKAGE

This has the advantage of all under one payment. Often these cars are still leased but this does not affect you. It can be an expensive option. Most of the big nationals do this and their fees can be in the £300+ a week bracket.

DRIVING SCHOOL AND CAR AS SEPARATE PACKAGE

Many schools will put you in touch with a lease company at a favourable term. This involves a simple credit check, and the lease companies say they can get anyone a car. All road tax and maintenance are provided in the package but watch out for things like tyres included. Some don't. The car is separate and if you wanted to change franchise, then the car goes with you. It's a very tax efficient way too and simpler on the accounts than purchasing.

DRIVING SCHOOL AND CAR TIED TO THE SCHOOL.

I saw this with a school a while ago. You signed up to the school for 24 months and had to take up a lease with their preferred car company on an 18-month lease. At the end of the 18 months, you signed another 18 months lease on a new car. This contract tied you to the school, so when your 24-month school franchise ran out, you were still tied because of the car. You had to renew your franchise and around it went again. They've gone bust now!!

Many Schools will let you use your own car if its suitable. I normally recommend using your own car if you can for the first 6 months as you start up. I also have a deal with lease companies that allows you to hand the car back early under certain circumstances.

The way some driving instructors hand their cars back after a lease would truly shock you, I hope. When I used to work for a large franchise, I saw a compound that contained several hundred cars that had come back off lease. Ripped upholstery that looks like a dog was burying a bone, filthy dirty, every panel damaged, cars burnt out, cars with batteries and other parts missing, to name a few things. Many were total write offs and this was from driving instructors driving. I used to always take pride in my vehicle and received several letters thanking me for how well looked after my vehicles were returned. I had the same when I was a service engineer too. A good driving instructor would surely take a pride in their vehicle.

I'VE HEARD THERE ARE TRAINING FEES, WHY AND HOW MUCH?

Almost all driving schools charge fees for training, not all do, and I'll come back to this later. Because all driving instructors are self-employed, the trainers who train driving instructors want paying. A small school wanting to expand might take on a trainee instructor but will charge for the time. Historically, a trainee instructor would have had around 50 hours of tuition and at £30 an hour, (being generous here because historically instructors were not paid that) would mean training fees of £1500.However you would often see training fees in the £3000 and in some cases £6000 so someone somewhere was making a large profit. Many of the larger schools used to make more money from training instructors than they did from the pupils. One large organisation was training 1000's yet had no driving school. Trainees were basically farmed off to the various driving schools. I have worked for both the large organisations and a driving school that benefited from the huge number of trainees coming from the organisation. It really was a sausage factory. Fortunately, those days are largely gone.

For many driving schools, they are not choosy who they take. If you have the money, they will take you on. At least for the training after all, you are a paying customer. There used to be a joke in the professions, 2 arms, 2 legs, £2000, you're in. Many totally unsuitable people started their training. Remember that large organisation? They would encourage you to pay on finance, interest free credit for one year. Telling you, that you'll be earning money long before the finance needs paying. So, the organization was paid by the finance company on day one. You now owed the finance company and on the 12-month anniversary, if you had not paid the loan in full, your £3500 training fee became almost £7000. I can't tell you how sad I felt with so many trainees crying on my shoulder because they were told they would be working before the 12 months. As an employed trainer, I had no control over this, my lesson slots were booked for me, trainees were waiting months between lessons, but as I say those days are gone, aren't they?

So, if you are paying fees, it's important to know what you are getting. An instructor trainer today, will want around £35-£45 an hour. Not all training is good, see the next section on training for more insight here. Also historically, there has been a high failure rate for trainee driving instructors. Driving Schools don't want to lose money so make the fees higher to cover losses. Trainees give up sometimes and it's important for you to think about how much you want to become a driving instructor before you start. You will have invested money in your future, and you don't want to waste it. You will hit that plateau in your training and the good trainer will guide you through it. I tell my trainers that the biggest battle with training is keeping the motivation going.

You may have read about me doing my master's degree in Driver Training Education. It was not all plain sailing. The study was hard, and I often sat there in front of a blank page, knowing I now had to write 3000 words on a subject, eventually, 12,000-word dissertation. So many times, I thought 'why am I bothering, why am I doing this to myself?'. I did not have to do it. Especially after completing my 12,000-

word dissertation plus many appendixes, submitting it for draft approval and being told most of it was not well written. I came so close to just chucking it all in the bin. After all, I only had 2-weeks and the final draft had to be submitted. Fortunately, I had a bit of inspiration from something else I was doing and understood, why it was not well written. In 2-weeks, I aced my viva (A presentation in front of three senior lecturers one of whom will try to rip my study to bits, it's their job) re-wrote my dissertation and was awarded my master's degree with Distinction. A very rare thing indeed.

Now even at £6000, the investment is good IF, you become a GOOD driving instructor. Make sure you know exactly what you are getting for your money. What if you do fail? Will they keep training you for free? Remember my own training I spoke about in an early chapter. I asked for another trainer and things changed.

SO WHY NOT FREE TRAINING?

Well, why not indeed. Since studying a lot about business and not so much about driving or teaching, I have learnt a lot about investment in business. I learnt about cost of acquisition and lifetime value etc. Now instructors and trainees are real people but driving schools are a business. Unfortunately, many run by people who are not or do not think like businesses. So, I had been asked a few times why driving schools charge and I always gave the same talk about self-employed etc. But it was over lock down when a friend asked me, and he said how he had recently had some more training with his company, and they just asked him to sign a contract to stay with them for 2 years. He had no intention of going anywhere anyway so he signed. And this got me thinking. So, during lock down for my school I started trialling a free training model. Now the risk is all mine. So, I interview (Zoom) potential instructors. I ensure we have demand in the areas, and I limit the number of trainees so the trainers can cope. We normally can get a trainee from start to earning in 3 months if they are dedicated. In return, I ask that instructors stay with me for at least 2 years after qualifying but as most of my instructors have tend to stay with me, this is something they would do anyway. To date, I think I am the only school to do this.

Let me tell you a funny little story to lighten the serious stuff. One day I was out giving driving lessons and I was on my second driving lesson of the day. Now remember I do two-hour lessons, so this is about my third hour into the day. I look down and notice I appear to have odd shoes on. Not slightly odd but one black and one brown shoe on. I stare for some time thinking this can't be right, as if they one will magically change colour. So, I pull my feet back and guide the pupil left and right until we get outside my own house. Hoping I can nip indoors to change before the pupil notices. I say to my pupil, please excuse me I need to go to the bathroom, and she says, 'I would change your shoes while you're there'. OMG the shock. I never found out if the first pupil of the day noticed.

CHAPTER 3: THE TRAINING

Introduction

This section deals primarily with the training of how to become a driving instructor and about what to look for and do when you first start. As I have said, I've spent over 20 years specifically on the training side, spent more money on qualifications than most and have taught easy ways to train for years. I truly believe anyone can become a driving instructor and those with the right attitude will become 'good' driving instructors. I think there is a difference between becoming a driving instructor and becoming a GOOD driving instructor. There is a wide variety of schools out there, all claiming they are the best. Only you can decide who is best and the ultimate decision is yours but do your homework. Consider where you do that homework too. Remember the Pareto Principle of 80% doing it wrong, even our top search engines are not programmed to give you the correct answers but the most popular. Much of what is written on the internet is from unqualified people. The driving profession is the same. Even some offering advanced courses and professional qualifications have themselves little in the way of actual educational or trade specific qualifications. Here's an interesting fact, to teach the part three, the teaching side of being a driving instructor, you legally need no qualifications whatsoever! Yes, that's right, not one single qualification is required in law to teach the part three. You do have to be a qualified driving instructor to teach the part two for money or monies worth, but not for part three. It is a shame that nearly all my colleagues who went on to do additional qualifications like degrees and Masters, went out to work in the fleet market or took jobs as fleet managers etc.

Do your research but check it carefully, there are some great salesmen out there!

ARE ALL DRIVING SCHOOLS THE SAME?

Well obviously not, but how do you choose the right school for your training? Don't chose by comparing prices. I have just read something that suggests we think of bulk as cheap and quality as expensive, but this is not necessarily so. Remember I talked about how some schools find they have too much work so think, hey I will train another instructor. Well, remember I told you I did my master's degree. Well, the final dissertation was about why training of driving instructors can be very poor. I spoke with many instructors, and I asked them the same questions.

1. What was your training like to become a driving instructor?
2. How is your training when training driving instructors?
3. What additional training have you done, to become an instructor trainer.

I will give you the responses to these questions below.

1. *What was your training like to become a driving instructor?*

Almost everyone said that their training was poor. Most had been trained by the same school and there were many examples of poor training. Most felt they were not ready to be an instructor after the training.

2. *How is your training when training driving instructors?*

Most said there training was a lot better although nobody could really give me specifics in how their training was better, they just felt it was better. My hypothesis was, they could not say because they had done nothing more to improve.

3. *What additional training have you done, to become an instructor trainer?*

An almost unanimous none. Yep none. And this was the problem. The reality was, they were copying the training they had as an instructor. They were giving the same 'rote' (learning by repetition) fixes to faults that they themselves would never do. They were using the same tools and techniques. Training was a laugh for them where they tried to role play the stupidest person, they could think of learning to drive. No wonder they could not answer question 2. And many of these were ORDIT trainers. (ORDIT is the Official Register of Driving Instructor Trainers and is widely promoted by the DVSA). There were of course exceptions. Trainer who did do training and reflected on their training each session to improve. Trainers that look for CPD, not only within the profession but outside. Looking for similar types of professional training. For the instructor trainer, we don't have to look far as ours is a skill of teaching. One of the reasons I took the professional teaching qualification.

So, choosing your school is difficult. Many schools still train instructors using the old Pre-set-tests (PST's) this was how the DVSA used to assess trainees with the examiner role playing 2 pupils of different standards over 10 pre-set-tests. So, there is the first start, does the school still use the PSTs to train? Training now is done where there is no PST and you are taught in part three to teach. Look for a school who tries not to separate the three tests, more later, who combine the tests and training more holistically. (As a whole and not separate) You know how to drive, you just need to know how to cascade this professionally to your pupils. So, let's look at how to become a driving instructor.

HOW TO BECOME A DRIVING INSTRUCTOR?

To become a driving instructor involves a bit of official paperwork and three tests. You must also register with the Driving and Vehicle Standards Agency (DVSA). To do this you must be over 21 years old and have held a driving licence for over three years, without holding any motoring convictions. You must also pass an enhanced Disclosure and Barring Service (DBS) check. You'll need to pass the ADI exam, which is in three stages, and you must pass all three to qualify:

ADI 1 – computer-based test in two parts; theory test and hazard perception test (You get unlimited attempts at this)

ADI 2 – practical test of driving skills (you are allowed three attempts at this)

ADI 3 – practical test of teaching ability (you are allowed three attempts at this)

Being a 'fit and proper' person

You must be a 'fit and proper' person to be an ADI.

The following is taken from the DVSA website,

'ADIs are in a position of considerable trust. The ADI Registrar protects the image of the register and maintains the public's confidence in the ADI industry.

What 'fit and proper' means

The law says you must be a 'fit and proper' person but does not define what it means.

The ADI Registrar interprets it as the personal and professional standards, conduct or behaviour that could be unacceptable in the eyes of the public and other ADIs.

It's not possible to be definitive about what's classed as 'fit and proper'. There must be some discretion to consider the circumstances of each case.

The ADI Registrar assesses the risk you're likely to pose to the public.' (DVSA, n.d.)

Personal conduct

When deciding if you're a 'fit and proper' person, the registrar will look at things such as motoring convictions, including fixed penalty notices. They will look at any periods of disqualification from driving and any court proceedings you may still have outstanding. As you might be working with under 18s or older who may be vulnerable, they need to know if you've ever been banned or barred from working with children under 18 years of age or had any substantiated complaints of inappropriate behaviour or misconduct. One thing they look at with particular interest is, have you ever had any substantiated complaints for financially inappropriate or fraudulent activity.

Normally this is a straightforward check, but I have had instructors come to me because of things in their past that worry them. I have helped them to become driving instructors and occasionally a covering letter to explain how something might be in the past and 'you have learnt the error of your ways' will help. I've never had one refused.

To start the process, go to the DVSA website through this link. https://www.gov.uk/become-car-driving-instructor

Assuming all is well, and it usually is, you will get a personal reference number (PRN) and you can now apply for your first test ADI 1. Often referred to as the theory test.

ADI 1 THEORY TEST

Now the popular way for this is to just sign up for an app and practice the questions. While this might get you a pass, it will not prepare you for the eventual training of learner drivers. It is of no use knowing that the stopping distance of a car at 30 mph is 'C'. I cannot stress this enough; you will need a more in-depth knowledge. Ideally, IF your trainer is teaching holistically, they will challenge you with questions while doing the in-car elements. A criticism I have of many instructors is, they just tell their learners to get on with their theory test and never actually use it in the lessons. A 'good' instructor will often ask 'what does the Highway Code say about this, or that?'. Getting pupils to 'understand' the rules. Your trainer should do this also. I have mentioned before, how worrying it is, seeing driving instructors ask basic questions in forums, and while you might question, why they ask it, the 20 different answers that follow are amazing. Often not one of them following the advice in the Highway Code.

THE TEST

The test itself is a two-part test,

- Multiple-choice questions
- Hazard perception test

MULTIPLE CHOICE QUESTIONS

You have 1 hour and 30 minutes to answer 100 multiple-choice questions.

Before the test starts, you'll get:

instructions on how the test works and the chance to do some practice questions to get used to the screens.

There are 25 questions in each of these 4 categories:

- road procedure
- traffic signs and signals, car control, pedestrians, and mechanical knowledge
- driving test, disabilities, and the law
- publications and instructional techniques

To pass you must get a minimum of 20% in each section and 85% overall.

So, 25 questions in each section, a minimum of 20 questions correct in each section BUT 85 questions correct overall. You might get 20 correct in every section but that's a fail, you need to be looking for 22 correct in every section really.

THE HAZARD PERCEPTION TEST (HPT)

Before you start the hazard perception test, you'll be shown a video about how it works.

You'll then watch 14 video clips.

The clips are showing everyday road scenes, and each contain at least one 'developing hazard' - but one of the clips features 2 developing hazards, you will not know which one.

You get points for spotting the 'developing' hazards as soon as they start to happen.

Now be careful as there is a difference between a 'potential' hazard and a 'developing' hazard.

Someone stood at a bus stop is a 'potential' hazard. If they go to walk out into the road in front of you, they are a 'developing' hazard. If you think of it as a film clip, everything up to the point before they go to move, scores 0 points, then as the move 5 points and gradually descending back to 0 again. This is one of the biggest failure points around this test with people clicking too early. Also remember, if you click too often, it will fail you.

Practice this with good software and you will understand.

To pass, there are a potential 75 points, and you need to get 57 or an average of 3.8 points per hazard.

You will be told at the test centre if you have been successful.

One of the bonuses of doing this test is, you will understand what your learner must do although their theory test is not so complex, and they can pass the HPT test with a lower score of 44 points from 75. It is the same test, just with a lower pass mark for pupils.

ADI 2 ABILITY TO DRIVE.

This test was historically a driving test and is still today positioned as a separate test by many schools and trainers. I mentioned earlier about the ADI 1 being treated separately. This test has been referred to as, an advanced test, when the truth is it is the same test as your learners will get however, this test is longer, and you're only allowed to make 6 driver faults or less. So, the test is the same, but the standard required is higher. Now I treat the training for this, and any good school should do too, holistically. I integrate it into the training. I refer to this as **'the standard you will demonstrate to your pupils'.** You're not showing the trainer how well you can drive; you are demonstrating what you will show and teach a learner driver. During your training, questions might be asked such as, 'how will you explain to a pupil what the turning point is'.

Often, I see advice such as 'you can do part 1 on your own and part 2 just get an instructor to brush up your driving'. With some driving schools, you would be better off doing this as you are just as likely 'not to pass' but to learn this properly all three parts of the qualifying process need to be integrated. Part one (ADI 1) is the knowledge you will give your pupil, part two (ADI 2) is the standard you will teach to and demonstrate and part three (ADI 3) is how you will teach it. I can't stress this enough but find a trainer that will integrate the three parts. You can pass the tests without but to be a truly good instructor, you need to understand how the three tests fit together. It's about the knowledge-the skill-the understanding.

THE TEST

To pass the test you must be able to:

- drive safely in different road and traffic conditions.
- show that you know The Highway Code by the way you drive.

You must bring:

- your UK driving licence.
- your approved driving instructor (ADI) part 1 pass certificate
- a suitable car

When you take a test, your car must:

- be taxed.
- be insured for a driving test (check with your insurance company)
- be roadworthy and have a current MOT (if it's over 3 years old)
- be a saloon, hatchback, or estate car in good working condition - you cannot use a convertible.
- have no warning lights showing, for example, the airbag warning light.
- have no tyre damage and the legal tread depth on each tyre - you cannot have a space-saver spare tyre fitted.
- be smoke-free - this means you cannot smoke in it just before or during the test.
- be able to reach at least 62mph and have a mph speedometer.
- have 4 wheels and a maximum authorised mass (MAM) of no more than 3,500 kg.

(DVSA, n.d.)

You can take your own vehicle, but you must supply an additional stick-on interior rearview mirror for the examiners use. More information can be found on the DVSA website https://www.gov.uk/adi-part-2-test/car-rules The test lasts about 1 hour.

There are 5 parts to the approved driving instructor (ADI) part two test:

- an eyesight check.
- 'Show me, tell me' Vehicle safety questions.
- general driving ability
- manoeuvres

Independent driving

The specifics of each part should be covered by your training school. I find in most circumstances, no more than 10-hours of tuition for this stage is required. A big problem is inexperienced trainers who try to teach trainees to drive. This is something I have found a lot in training with novice instructors thinking they are going to have to give trainees 40+ hours of tuition. I try to remind them that the trainee CAN drive, they are STILL alive, and it is just a matter of coaching back to the standard, and a little beyond they once did. Experienced trainers find 6-hours of tuition is not uncommon to be thinking there is little else to teach and it's just a mock test.

ADI 3 ABILITY TO TEACH.

This is the subject I based my degrees on, the subject I have spent over 20 years working on. Long before the DVSA abandoned the pre-set-tests, (PST's) I had stopped them, favouring real teaching of lessons. I knew that part three (ADI 3) was not about the rote teaching of every lesson but about teaching instructors to 'teach'.

I attended night school to study for my City and Guilds certificate in education Alongside me were, yoga teachers, electrical engineering teachers, art teachers and even a probation officer. Were we taught how to teach our individual subjects? No! we were taught how to teach the subjects we already have expert understanding of. At part three, you have already demonstrated your theory knowledge and practical skill. You have demonstrated that you have 'expert knowledge'. Part three is how to cascade those things you are an expert in.

Still today I see trainers trying to teach trainees to do individual lessons giving fixes to faults that they would never use in their own driving. You might be lucky to pass this way, but you'll never properly understand how to teach when new things come up. This probably why we have so many instructors on social media asking, 'how do I teach this'. You know, after all you would know what to do if YOU were driving (I hope), part three should teach you how to cascade everything you do and know to your pupil. It does not mean that everything you do needs to be taught. Once you know the process, the rest is easy. Could you imagine trying to teach a pupil on every road in the UK just in case they use it? No! We teach a few roads and how to cascade this to roads they don't yet know, or that's the theory anyway.

So, the answer was that the training had to change, and change dramatically. It needed to stop being about the 'fault based' method and more about teaching life skills. 'Goal based'. Changing to a more coaching based training rather than telling. This has caused a lot of talk in the profession. Many still do not understand the objects of coaching, some just do not want to change, and others mystify it into some secret art. There is no secret to coaching, you probably do it every day. 'Where did I put my keys?' could be answered with 'where did you last have them?' This causes the person to think about where they could be and often this finds them. It also suggests that they did not keep them where they normally would and next time, they might put them back in the right place. A learning process has gone on. Telling them, 'They are on the bedside cupboard' does little but teach them that next time they want their keys, to ask you again, and again, and again. Go back to my signal scenario earlier on. Just telling them, 'Yes signal here', teaches them to ask you every time and no real learning is taking place.

Do not try and rehearse a lesson with a pupil.

THE TEST

There is not time in this book to go through all you need to know about the training, that is another whole book. I have some excellent resources I have written on this including a complete course here https://dte-elite.co.uk/a-comprehensive-guide-to-train-the-trainer/ . The test should be explained in your training. Here I will outline some important things for you to get a feel for what you should expect.

For the test, you will be expected to take a pupil to teach something. You will deliver a real lesson to a pupil. Now this does not have to be an actual pupil. You can take along a friend or member of the family and teach them something. In my experience, this often goes badly wrong as the proper pupil-teacher relationship is not there. I know an instructor who took their husband and he started to argue through the test. He started questioning her and the wife (Instructor) struggled where she wouldn't have with a pupil. (They are divorced now) Another took her daughter, and the daughter had a bit of a tantrum causing mum to go into mum mode and started arguing back. Even I tried to teach my own daughter to drive many years ago, nope, I just could not. So, I say, take a real learner. Fortunately, there is a system in place called the trainee licence scheme designed for you to get practice with real pupils, before taking the test. This means you will have a few pupils to choose from and with your trainer, you can discuss the best option with the most suitable pupil. I always say, don't take you hardest pupil and don't take your easiest pupil. Take someone who will communicate with you and someone who you can teach something to.

Do not try and rehearse a lesson with a pupil. I see a very common question on social media is, 'what's the best lesson for the part three test?' My answer is always, the one the pupil is ready for, the one you would do anyway even if this was not the part three test and the one the pupil needs most. I see instructors trying to take pupils on the route and rehearse questions they will ask for the test. Examiners will see straight through this. And anyone who has done my training will know my golden rule, **the pupil will regress back at least 3 lessons.** Yes, suddenly, the MSPSL routine that they have never missed before is forgotten, or suddenly they don't know how to use the clutch or brake. Yes, it happens, and it is a huge bonus. Really you think! Yes, because it gives you a chance to change the lesson plan to meet the needs of the pupil. This is one of the required standards you will need to meet.

There are 17 things, known as competencies, you will need to meet under three headings (see appendix 1)

- lesson planning
- risk management
- teaching and learning strategies.

LESSON PLANNING

This is about how well you plan the lesson. Not just the initial lesson planning but during the lesson. If you see a fault or see something that needs attention, how you change the plan to deal with it.

RISK MANAGEMENT

Keeping the pupil, yourself, and other road users safe always is paramount always. This is about how you were aware of what is going on not just in the car but outside too. Being aware of your surroundings. Identifying risks and planning how you will deal with them.

TEACHING AND LEARNING STRATEGIES.

Briefly, this is how you conduct the lesson, what styles you use and how well you communicate with your pupil. You need good rapport when delivering a driving lesson with your pupil.

As I have said, this book has not the space to deal with all the training, but further advice and information can be found for free on my website https://dte-elite.co.uk/

Each of the competencies are marked on the test from 3 down to 0 and you need a minimum of 31 for a pass. The grades are given below.

- 0-30, Fail: Your performance is unsatisfactory, and you will not join the ADI register.
- 31-42, Grade B: You'll be allowed to join the ADI register.
- 43-51, Grade A: You have shown a high standard of instruction and you'll be allowed to join the ADI register.

It is worth noting that a score of 7 or less in the risk management section will result in an automatic fail.

TRAINING ADVICE

It is vital that your training is about these competencies, so you fully understand how to apply each one and how they fit together. A weakness in one, can easily cascade across others. For example, a failure to spot a serious fault will obviously give you a low score there but will also affect your score on, ability to change the lesson plan, and meeting the needs of the pupil etc. Of course, the opposite is true. If you meet the needs of the pupil, you are identifying risks and probably changing the plan to suit. This is where the skill of your trainer can help as by working on the right competencies, they can dramatically lift many other sections.

Like to other two tests, you will be given your result on the day. After this test the examiner will go off for around 10-15 minutes to look at their notes and check the scores. They will return and after asking your pupil to take a seat in a waiting room or moving you to the waiting room, will give you a debrief.

Important note.

Take this debrief as positive, whatever the outcome. If you fail, they will be telling you what you need to do to pass, if you pass, there will be information to help you gain a stronger grade at a further check later. Listen loosely and IF your trainer is not with you, as soon as possible relay the information to your trainer. Keep notes if you prefer.

TRAINING SUPPORT

During training, our trainees get a chance to'.

- Learn the theory of each subject.
- Demonstrate how they will teach driving.
- Observe several real lessons given by a qualified instructor (sitting in the back)
- Plan many different lesson types and have them assessed by an instructor.
- Deliver driving lessons to role playing instructors.
- Deliver driving lessons or parts to real pupils, with an instructor observing (it really is different with a pupil)

The above covers many aspects of learning types and gives a real all round (holistic) way of training. Make sure who ever trains you gives you all these opportunities.

Let us lighten the mood a little with a couple of funny stories told to me by a London examiner about two part three tests. The first the examiner had explained he was going to role play a pupil for a turn in the road lessons. (this was the old style test some years ago). As with any turn in the road lesson, it was typical for the examiner to role play clutch problems on the initial drive. The examiner moves off in role and brings the clutch up too fast causing the car to jerk off quickly. The PDI warns him to bring it up better as he will break his car. No assistance was given so the examiner did it again. The PDI then firmly tells the examiner (remember the examiner is role playing a pupil) don't do it again, adding he did not care how he drove his own car, but he was to drive his with more respect.

The examiner, still in role, says he's finding it difficult and thinks he needs some help. (a massive hint from the examiner) None was forthcoming, so the examiner tries it again. This time the PDI threatened to give the examiner a slap if he did it again. The examiner abandoned the test for his safety.

On the 2nd story, the examiner role playing a pupil doing a reverse round the corner, stated he could not see behind very well. The examiner expected the PDI to explain he could shift in his seat a little to help see behind but no, the PDI wound down the window and decided to get out the car and guide the examiner back from outside the car. Now this of course would be illegal with a real learner and hence he failed.

THE TRAINEE LICENCE SCHEME (PDI)

I have mentioned above, the trainee licence scheme also known as a pink licence (pink). It is known as a 'pink' because the badge is pink in colour. The trainee licence scheme is a way of getting additional practice while working as a driving instructor. Whilst you can earn money on this scheme, it is important to remember it is more about practice. To me, it's invaluable practice and a chance for your trainer observe you delivering real driving lessons. They can give you advice on how to make them better. It gives you a chance to reflect on your lessons and compare them to the competencies you must use for your test. This licence has great advantages when used correctly but it can have a huge problem if you do not use it correctly. I cover this in the next section. The DVSA have been talking about using a reflective log or workbook for years. They even gave a date that they would release one but that was 4 years back and no log has been seen. They always stated that instructors and schools will be able to use their own and I produced one for trainees many years ago. This is a great way for you to record your thoughts and what you 'feel' you have learnt. It is or should not be about your command of the English, or whatever language you use, quality nor about handwriting. Used properly, it is a very valuable tool. I hear many examiners ask for them now at part three tests. You can't fail or even be marked down for not having one (at the time of writing) but, how will you feel if you are asked, and you don't have one? ALL my trainees have one and their feedback sheets and reflective notes are all inside. Now whilst the examiner is not going to read it all, imagine what they are already thinking when you produce one!

To be able to go on the trainee licence scheme, you must have completed 40 hours of training, and this must be logged. It does not all have to be in-car. The DVSA requirement is that a minimum of 25% must be in-car. You must be sponsored by a driving school and together with the driving school you apply for the trainee licence through the DVSA. The current fee can be found at https://www.gov.uk/approved-driving-instructor-adi-fees

While on your trainee licence you have two options, a training route where you must have an additional 20 hours of training (25% minimum in-car again) or the supervision route where you must be, supervised for 20% of your lessons.

The scheme gives you a chance to practice all the things you have learnt. To reflect and refine the competencies until you're confident. You can ask your trainer questions on points you do not understand and can gain in confidence and rapport with your pupils. However, let's look at where this can go wrong.

HOW THE TRAINEE LICENCE CAN GO WRONG

Many trainees, get their licence and just start teaching their way. They ignore the things they were taught and just start delivering lessons. I have sat in on 100's of trainee instructors and I nearly always see the same thing. No lesson plan, no goals set, and it seems as if they are just going for a drive with the pupil and talking about the odd fault. Driving lessons must be goal focused and not fault focused. EVERY lesson has a goal you are looking to achieve.

The next fault I continually see is, not changing the lesson plan. A goal is set to maybe 'recap on roundabouts.' But from the back I see the pupil struggling with something basic like clutch control. The trainee instructor continues with the lesson either not mentioning the clutch or paying lip service to it, 'remember the clutch' is often all that is said. You need to change the goal to clutch and make a mini plan to sort the clutch fault. All that's needed is probably 10-15 minutes working on the clutch then returning to the original goal of roundabouts, but now with the clutch sorted.

Case study

I took an instructor out recently. He did a vague asking the pupil what they wanted to do today. The pupil who drove extensively with her parents said 'her road position and roundabouts'. So off we went. Now the lesson started in Callington and the instructor wanted to do the lesson in Launceston. Callington is some 10 miles away. I am sitting quietly in the back. For the whole journey to Launceston and for that matter back to Callington, the pupil could not keep the car in a straight line. We moved from left to right with not a word said about it from the instructor. Every now and again he would pop up with 'what does that sign mean?' Unfortunately, we had passed the sign before he finished saying this. If you don't know yet, most positioning faults come from the eyes, where the pupil is or in this case not looking. The pupil was simply not looking down the road far enough (very common fault in novice pupils). The instructor was making the problem worse by identifying signs far too late. Causing the pupil to look even closer. To make matters worse, almost every time this pupil braked, she was almost putting us through the windscreen. Not one mention of this was made of this either.

In the above case study, the instructor was not dealing with the needs of the pupil. In order, the instructor should have sorted the brakes first and then moved on the stated goal of position, he felt that because he was asking questions, that was ok. He was filling the lesson but with the wrong stuff. Not meeting the needs of the pupil. 'Fill the lesson with the lesson' I often say. If you're working on mirrors, then talk about mirrors not other stuff.

The main problem is trainees do not follow what they have been taught. I am referring to them being taught properly because there are still instructors, qualified for many years who teach just like the case study.

I produced a lesson planner for instructors that should help them. It uses a lesson plan guide on one side and the diagram on the other side to help pupils. Used correctly, it will help until the teaching process becomes automatic. You can see this planner here. https://dte-elite.co.uk/product/lesson-planner/

If you practice something wrong, all you do is re-enforce this. You need to make sure everything is practised the right way, so it soon becomes second nature. A lot of trainees teach their own way when with the pupils, then try to teach the right way with the trainer. A good trainer sees it a mile off! Practice and reflect and you WILL be successful.

THE PLATEAU

I want you to remember this section well. During your training to be a driving instructor, YOU WILL HIT A PLATEAU. It happens to everyone. You will recognise it by you wondering if you will ever pass or wonder why you ever started. You'll try to convince yourself it's not for you or something similar. It happened to every successful driving instructor out there, it happened to me! It does not just affect driving instructors. When doing my masters, still up at 2am and writing, I would ask myself 'David, why are you putting yourself through this?' I have mentioned before in my training to be a driving instructor, I was convinced I could not do it. I went to see another trainer who told me how experienced she was. She looked at my training and said 'David, you will NEVER make it as a driving instructor'. I so almost gave up. Incidentally, she was sitting in the audience when I was awarded my Diploma in Driving Instruction Dip.DI. There is a photograph on the day where I am shaking the hand of Pam Barnaville MA,Dip.DI who was presenting the award. I am looking straight at the woman who said I would never make it. She never spoke to me again...

When you hit the plateau, recognise it as that and push on. I'm glad I did, and I am sure you will be too.

PASSING THE PART 3, OR FOR THAT MATTER A STANDARDS TEST IS EASY!

An old story

It must be over 15 years since I penned an article of almost the same title. This article is the updated version of that one. When I say updated, most of it is still true today and the mysteries of passing these tests are nothing more than following the simple rules. The rules are laid out by the DVSA in their Standards for driving instructors, but this can all look very daunting to the new instructor. Let me begin.

Part three, and when I say part three, take it to mean the standard test too, is NOT about impressing the examiner. It is not about delivering YOUR best lesson. It is not even about how many qualifications you have or don't have. It's not about your car or where you live. There is no right or wrong pupil. It's not about how social media forums will have you believe about 'don't do manoeuvres' or 'don't do this'.

What it is about is delivering a lesson to a pupil that meets the needs of that pupil here and now. I get asked on a regular basis, 'what's the best lesson for my part three test?' It will be met every time with the same answer, one that meets the learners needs now. My advice normally follows with, whatever time your test is, look for a pupil who would normally have that lesson time, teach them whatever you would have taught them on that lesson normally.

GROW AND
GROW AGAIN.

Now the above advice is a little simplistic in that we must assume that you are normally delivering a proper driving lesson. One that you set goals with the pupil and recap the prior learning to assess if this lesson is reasonable. A normal lesson would have you asking pupils 'how would they like you to teach them today and ensuring the pupil knows how you will both share the responsibility. One of the best methods I know of doing this, is by using the GROW model.

GROW IS COVERED A LOT IN MY VIDEOS AND ARTICLES BUT TO RECAP FOR THE PURPOSES OF THIS SECTION OF THE BOOK,

Goals: EVERY lesson, we set and establish a goal for the lesson, something that is achievable, give the time frame of the lesson. These are usually pupil led. Simply ask them what they would like to achieve today. If you are using a progress record that you tick off after every lesson, the pupil will have a good idea what they need to do today.

Realistic: Is the goal you have chosen realistic? A quick question and answer session of knowledges that they would done previously that can support this goal. For example, if this is their first manoeuvre, then clutch control and hill starts maybe. Draw out the sub skills so they know they already know part of today's lesson. This is often called **the transfer of skills.**

Options: ASK THEM, how would they like to do this lesson today, don't assume you're getting out the lesson planner and going to give them a 7.36-minute briefing (or whatever time your trainer told you a briefing should last!) followed by guided, prompted practice. Maybe they fancy a change today, probably not but give them the option. Different pupils respond better to different teaching methods. Different lessons transfer better using different methods. Essentially, it's pupil led so ask them.

Way forward: Having set a goal, worked out it's realistic and found out how your pupil would like to be taught today, set out your plan. 'So, in the next 20-minutes we will........................' Give it a time frame, ask them how would they like to share the responsibility, what help would they like? Let them know you're there if they need you. In early lessons this might be 'I have the dual controls if needed' and in later lessons that might be 'I will only say anything if I see something wrong'. A great way to do this is to use scaling. Asking a pupil how confident they feel from 1 to 10. If a pupil says 5, then you are going to get them to 7,8, or 9 by the end of this lesson.

Now this whole GROW process takes just a few minutes,

and you need to do this EVERY lesson, so it becomes natural not just for you but your pupils. As you become more experienced, it becomes no more difficult than the well-practiced, 'hello, how are you today? Parents, OK?' We ask these things automatically and in reality; they are just words with no real feeling often.

Get into the habit of using the GROW model every lesson.

AN ALL-TOO-
COMMON STORY.

If you use the GROW model, many of the 17 Standards set out by the DVSA are covered. Then it's just about delivering the lesson as it happens. One of the most common things I say is 'deal with the here and deal with it now'. You all have the skills to deal with every situation but often we defer it. Let me give you a most common example. Many of you will recognise this and if you do, be brave and reflect on them.

> You're delivering a lesson when you see something simple going wrong, something you know your pupil knows how to do yet they seem to not be doing it. Mirrors is an example of this. You maybe give it a brief mention like 'don't forget your mirrors' but you carry on with your main lesson, puzzled by why your pupil is not doing it. You keep plugging away at the original lesson goal, partly distracted by the strange out of character fault and partly by hoping the examiner has not seen the fault. (they have by the way). You may make mention, often in the debrief at the end as to 'we will look at that next week'.

Now I am sure this is so familiar to many in many forms. Let's look at it from the back, from the examiners point of view.

Lesson going well, oh some mirror faults, ok. Umm instructor has made a brief reference to them but why are they not dealing with it? Umm mirrors are a basic skill, why is this not being picked up? It's dangerous not to be checking mirrors. OK nice manoeuvre being taught, I like the transfer to the reference points but hey, what about the basics, the mirrors? Oh, that was disappointing, they would have passed if they had delt with that safety critical point, I'll give them some advice and will see them next time. Shame!

There may be examiners reading this too who might recognise this type of scenario.

And let's not forget our pupil, what are they thinking.

OMG is this man in the back watching me? Damn, I think I forgot my mirror, its ok my instructors not noticed as they said nothing. Hopefully the man in the back missed it too, damn and another one, why is my instructor not saying anything, they usually do and why do they look so nervous? I wonder if I will get this man in the back as my examiner on my test, oh I'm struggling to concentrate today...

Deal with the here and deal with it now, if you deal with it straight away, then all is well. Let's try again.

Ah you missed you mirror there, what mirrors should you use, ah you're not sure, that ok let's have a little chat. Let's set a mini **goal** based on the mirrors, (ask a few mirror related questions, **Realistic**) How shall we do this, shall we go back around the block and we practice the mirrors? (**Options**) Ok then for the next 5 minutes lest just concentrate on the mirrors again (**way forward**) ...

5 minutes on and, brilliant so let's go back to our original goal of....................

In the last scenario, everyone is happy, the examiner sees a refreshing change, they see the pupil sort a fault. They know that if you can sort this one out you can sort anything out. The pupil feels happy because you are in charge and they are learning, and you will be and feel in charge. A win-win-win situation.

So, to recap, use the GROW model every lesson, and deal with the here and now and strangely the rest will take care of itself to some degree.

SUMMARY

There is nothing to worry about in the qualifying tests. For years trainees have been worried about passing and they should not. My specialist subject has always been about showing how easy these tests are. Over the years I have rescued 1000's who were finding it difficult and with one day with me, they would go away saying, surely it can't be that easy, yes, it is!

There are three parts to the qualifying test. A theory, a practical drive, and an ability to teach. It is important to take training that will treat the three parts as a whole and teach you holistically. The debrief at the end of any test is valuable and geared towards improving things. Choose your trainer carefully and use my guide above to help you. Try to find someone who uses a reflective workbook of some form, you might not feel like using one but trust me, it helps. I have shown that even within driving schools, trainers can be different. Don't be afraid to ask for another trainer.

CHAPTER 4:
WORKING AS
A DRIVING
INSTRUCTOR.

This chapter looks at some of the things you need to consider now you are qualified. There have been many instructors who, when qualified felt they were left to fend for themselves. Historically, these were the ones who passed, and their trainers would now make no more money from them. Remember, driving schools would often make their money from the training fees. So, this section gives you just some of the information you will need to ensure your journey continues to be a successful one.

ADI REGISTER

Once you have passed all three parts of the qualifying exam, you'll be able to apply for your Approved Driving Instructor badge (ADI). The badge lasts four years, after which you must renew the badge with a fresh DBS check. You can do this using the link in the following section. This is a green colour badge and sometimes referred to as 'green badge'. If you have some time left on your trainee badge, you don't have to apply for it straight away. This can save you a few pounds if you have a few months left. Now just because you have your green badge it is important to still think about training. The examiner on your part three test, will still have given you advice. It used to be the case that you would normally be invited, (I love the term 'invited' like you have a choice) for a 'standards check', (covered in next section) within six months but in these strange post covid times, this has gone a bit array. Do not forget to keep delivering lessons the way you were shown and the way you passed your test. Many instructors don't continue with the way they passed their test. They slip into bad habits, and then panic when they get their Standards Check. In the early days it is about perfecting those lesson skills and gaining rapport with your pupils. The problem is, you have no boss giving you a monthly appraisal, nobody is really watching you if you go wrong. Now this might seem like a dream job, but your critics and appraisals are given by each pupil. Not to you directly but indirectly by your pupils telling you something like 'I'm having a lesson break for a bit' or 'I can't afford my lessons for a few weeks, I'll call you'. There are a lot of reasons like this given and while a few of them might be genuine, in 20+ years I know most are not genuine. It is easy to make excuses too, blaming offers or the school you work for losing pupils, but the school has been doing this a long time and will have others in the same area not losing pupils. Remember I said earlier, most pupils leave their instructor because they don't feel like they're making progress or some other reason.

Let's imagine you just passed your part three with a 31-35 score. In truth, you passed but only just. If you deviate at all from how you delivered your part three test, you will immediately fall in the below 30 scoring zone, a fail. If you don't do any CPD or even reflection on how you are delivering driving lessons, your grade will be falling. Nobody is going to tell you. There is nobody watching your lessons. No critic, apart from I mentioned, the pupil. How will you know? You won't, But the day that letter drops on your doorstep inviting you to a Standard Check, you know how you are going to feel. Now if your training is sub-standard, and don't blame the DVSA system, you are going to worry. I and many of my trainers often see someone who has failed 2 Standard Checks and only ask for help the week before the third and final. Then expect a miracle. There are certain things a good trainer can do to help you through the test but like wrapping an exhaust bandage around a hole in your exhaust, it is a temporary fix.

You don't need to pay out for lots of expensive training if you keep up to date. There are several online CPD zoom calls, some are good, some not so but have a look around and see what feels right for you. I run them myself almost every week, free of charge. No ulterior motive, just to help instructors and a place they can come and ask questions and get facts. I certainly won't try and sell you a course or anything. Its my way of giving back.

If your school offers additional training, sometimes called CPD (Continuing professional development), make time to do it. As a driving school owner, myself, I run additional CPD for many things. Lesson structure, rapport, how to get you pupils to stay with you even if they don't like you, and many other things. Schools like mine run courses normally free to help their instructors to be better instructors. A bad instructor is not good for a school. So, make the time for these courses and gradually your test passes will increase, and you will have happier pupils.

CPD is for life, not just for Christmas.

Integrated register of driver trainers (IRDT)

Driving instructors have a link to their online information kept on them. It contains some very useful services.

You can use this service to:

- apply for trainee licence to give driving instruction.
- apply for your first ADI registration certificate.
- track the progress of your ADI registration.
- renew your ADI registration.

Registered ADIs can use this service to amend their details held on the training and registration system, and to:

- register for Continuing Professional Development (CPD)
- register to be a Pass Plus instructor.
- Order a pass plus starter or refill pack.
- Change your contact and personal details.
- View customer certificate numbers.
- View your check test and badge status including fleet, ORDIT etc.

http://www.businesslink.gov.uk/bdotg/action/detail? itemId=1082201911&type=PIP

This page links you to instructor online services from the Driving Standards Agency (DSA).

If you do not have or have lost your log in details, then email IRDT@dsa.gsi.gov.uk
Provide any 2 from the following and they will send you log on details.
ADI number (PRN)
Driver number (Licence number)

Date of birth

STANDARDS CHECK

As I write this, the DVSA have just announced the changes in the way a driving instructor will be called for their Standards Check. Rather than the four-yearly call-up that we've all gotten used to, the DVSA are now going to use the following criteria, each one known as a trigger. I've listed them below:

Average number of driving faults per test @ 5 or greater

Average number of serious faults per test @ 0.5 or greater

The percentage of driving tests where the driving examiner had to take physical action @ 10% or higher

Driving test pass rate @ 55% or lower

The first thing to point out is that each trigger on its own will not lead to early standards check. Over a 12-month rolling period, at least 3 out of 4 of these triggers will need to be activated to be called for a check by the DVSA. This is great news, and something needed for some time to account for so many instructors who present pupils for test too early.

If you get 3 out of 4 of these triggers, the first instance you will receive a telephone call from a DVSA enforcement officer. This is a rather official title for what we once knew were SEADI's. The role of the enforcement officer is a bridge between Driving Instructor and the DVSA. They are usually ex driving instructors who have taken additional training by the DVSA. You will get a call to discuss what you can do to improve your test pass statistics. If you teach a lot of special needs pupils, this should be discussed as it could have a bearing on your results. This is a call to help and support you if you need it. There are many driving instructors who specialise in special needs pupils. Although it could be argued that as a special needs teacher, you will know how many additional driving lessons each pupil will need to meet their needs. In any event you might be asked to do a Standard Check test where the examiner will need to observe one of your driving lessons with a pupil.

The need for this recent change in the standard test requirement has been brought about by the very low pass rate of pupils for their driving test. There is a strange statistic that shows, pupils presented for a driving test taught by parents etc, is higher than when presented for test with a driving instructor. At the time of writing, test pass averages were around 53%, pre-lockdown it was 46%. It does differ between areas; however, this is still and has been a very worrying trend for many years. My belief is a combination of driving instructors underestimating their pupil's ability for actual test and the perceived financial constraints of a pupil who puts the instructor under pressure for an early test. Following this standard test section, I go into a little more detail under 'preparing your pupil to fail a test'. Yes, I did say preparing your pupil to FAIL a test!

Your Standards Check will be carried out just like your part three test. The DVSA will send you an invitation for your Standards Check, this can be changed and on the day an examiner will sit in one of your driving lessons for about 40 minutes. At the end they will give you your result. The pass mark is just like the part three 0-30 is a fail, 31-42 will be grade B and 43-51 grade A.

In theory, you should get one Standard Check in each four-year registration period. However, you can be called in early if you have a low-test pass rate with your pupils or maybe complaints are made about you. Your pupils may be getting a lot of faults in one area, and this might trigger an early test. This is a good thing as it alerts you to any potential problems that could potentially damage your business.

There is a lot of criticism about this test. In my opinion it is because too many driving instructors do very little having passed part three and start to panic. But you get three attempts at this Standards Check and nobody should ever fail all three if they take training. None of my own instructors have ever failed this Standard Check system but then I offer free training and they can always come to me for advice. My speciality has always been about how simple all this process is. The advice given in part three applies here and the advice here applies in part three. All you need to do is show a good driving lesson, with good planning and that the pupil has learnt something. You do this using those 17 competencies again. (Appendix 1). Take a pupil who will talk to you and is not afraid to ask questions. Take a pupil who you can teach something to. Often, I see the plan is something like 'to consolidate roundabouts.' They mean to improve on their roundabouts but so many things can go wrong elsewhere. In this scenario, the pupil is probably responsible for everything else also. This is where things will go wrong. They will mess up in clearance, or a junction or anything else and the instructor will miss it, the examiner in the back will not though. My advice is taking a more novice pupil, someone who you are still developing their driving. Someone where you will be taking responsibility for other things. Keeping it simple works well here.

My own first Standards check (known as a check test back then), did not quite go as planned. I took a pupil who had just failed her test on the reverse left, although had some driver faults for anticipation. So, this was my goal. It was soon apparent that out of the test centre, my pupil was not using her MSPSL routine (A routine you will learn in your training). But I kept on with trying to improve her anticipation. I'm asking her, what might happen here and what there etc. The mirrors were particularly missing. When I did mention them, she responded with 'I never got a fault on them on my test so they must be ok'. This somewhat threw me. While continuing with the lesson, I knew it was all going wrong, so I pulled her over. I had a stern chat about mirrors etc and at the end we agreed we would spend a little time on this aspect. Unfortunately, I did not but proceeded to continue with anticipation. The result was an Educational, back then you did not get a fail on your first check test but it was marked 'E' as educational. My only fault was I did not do what I said I would do. 60 minutes later and her mirrors were still poor. I never made the mistake again.

In my own check test, the examiners advice was fantastic. He spent around 20 minutes with me pointing out aspects that I could improve my teaching. This was like my appraisal I suppose. I set about improving and became a better instructor. Many instructors do not use this advice as advice but rather criticism and seem to reject it. They come out fighting like a wounded dog. My advice is to look at the Standard Check like this. An examiner with years of experience will sit in the back of one of your lessons. At the end, they will give you some of the best advice going for free. Of course, a good idea is to get someone to sit in your lessons before the examiner does and look. This is something I do for my instructors and gives them a chance to work on things before the examiner sees it.

PREPARING YOUR PUPIL TO FAIL THE TEST.

The above title seems a little negative, but this is in fact what many instructors do without realising it. Every pupil who takes a driving test needs to be able to drive without an instructor having to say anything for at least the duration of every driving lesson. Not just the one driving lesson before but at least six driving lessons before. In theory you should be able to hold a light conversation about anything but driving or perhaps the higher levels of driving such as why things could be different or what might change in the future. In many instances, driving instructors, are often still pointing out things and correcting faults, right up to the driving test. Instructors are simply not sharing the responsibility. Oh! That sounds like one of the 17 competencies!

Driving examiners use a standard language for route direction and manoeuvres, yet so often I hear driving instructors use a different system. Following the guidance in DT1, the driving examiners code, easily downloadable, will eliminate these confusions. Pupil get used to hearing an instructor use phrases like 'hang a right ere' or 'not that one, this one', when they hear the proper wording, it puts them off. I have even heard complaints on forums about why the examiners do not talk like the instructors. I hope you agree, the good driving instructor would use the uniform wording to help prepare the pupils. We've all heard of the 'three-point turn'! well it's never been called that officially. An examiner would ask a pupil to 'turn the vehicle in the road using the forward and reverse gears.' Many pupils would not know what the examiner was talking about, whose fault is that? You need to give instruction clearly and concisely. Oh! That also sounds like a competency!

Mock tests are a valuable way of not only assessing your pupil's readiness but also going a long way to helping with nerves, if the test is conducted with realism, feels official and exactly like a real test. If the mock test is like a normal lesson where you keep talking and do not give it 'realism, then it is of little value. I would do these mock tests and only give the minimum talk in the car, just route directions etc. After I would ask pupils how they felt, and they usually say it was scary. They knew that the driving was down to them, and they had to cope.

At least six weeks before a driving test I would always ask my pupils this. 'If your driving test was today, what would you be worried about?' They would always tell me, and then that's what we would cover. It was interesting how many of my pupils passed yet were disappointed. Why disappointed, because they never got to show the things six weeks ago, they were then most scared of. It is then that you know they are ready.

Then there is the day of the test. A good driving instructor will ensure they have their driving licence, theory test certificate (yes, I know the examiner rarely asks for it) and their confirmation email or letter. A bottle of water is a useful tip too so they can sip before the test. Arrive at the test centre and relax your pupil, ask them about anything but the driving. I used to spend a lot of time, not just entertaining my pupils but the pupils who had been abandoned by their own instructors as they went off to chat to their mates. They will want the toilet, so take their documents and the keys and hold them for them else they leave them in the toilet.

If pupils have anything they are worried about on their driving test, imagine what's going through their mind sitting in that test centre. They are worried they are going to go left toward that roundabout they hate, or down to the area where they do the reverse park. Whatever their worry is, it will be going through their mind hoping they do not get 'this or that'. Therefore, I do the question six weeks before, let's get it out of the system, lets sort those worries and difficulties so they are not hoping they will pass, they are knowing they can.

I mentioned earlier those instructors often feel it's all about money. Look at how many pupils will ask you nearer their test time 'if you have any gaps or cancellations, can they do extra driving lessons'. It is about trust and knowing that you are giving them honest advice. If you do the above correctly, they will know you are doing your best for them. You will be preparing them not only to pass but to be independent drivers, for life.

WHAT TYPE OF DRIVING SCHOOL SHOULD I WORK FOR?

There is always a lot of debate about who a driving instructor should work for. There is a lot of hostility on driving school forums towards franchises. I believe a lot of this is because sometimes instructors feel they were let down by one of the poorer franchises and partly because, well, they don't like the competition. I have said this many times but too many driving instructors are not business minded and their only way to market is to knock the competition. An independent driving instructor can have many strengths but if business is not one of them, then don't do it. There are basically three types of driving instructor. Franchised, independent and employed.

FRANCHISED

It is worth noting that the term 'franchise' in the driver world, is not a true franchise as it rarely follows a set up as recognised by the British Franchising Association. It is however widely accepted as a term within the profession so for simplicity stakes, I will continue to use it.

You work for a driving school on a self-employed basis keeping all the lesson payments but pay the driving school a weekly franchise fee. They, in principle, do all your marketing, branding and pupil supply. They will usually have an office and staff who answer the phones and allocate pupils to you using an online diary. Sometimes they offer training and additional services but not always. The main reason for being with a franchise is it's a 'done for you service'. For it to work well, you need to believe in the school or franchise you work for. That they offer a good service to you and a good service to your pupils. When you are proud to work for the franchise, you work with, it works very well for all parties.

INDEPENDENT

As an independent instructor, you would do all your own marketing and branding, sourcing pupils, answering the phone and everything involved. You would have to source any training independently and pay for it. You become a driving school in your own right. If you set this up properly and you're in the right area, this can work very well. Pupils will like you and trust you and the business can boom. It takes a lot of hard work to do it correctly but done right, it can work out very well. Once you have finished lessons though, you then have the admin and everything else to do. What often happens when driving instructors go independent is they start to drop many of the services they had with a franchise. They stop doing licence checks, don't take out liability insurances and don't offer card payments to name a few. Gradually they slip down a slide where they will blame pupils and everyone else when things go wrong. They sometimes start using the phone during lessons to take messages as they don't want to miss pupils. It takes a lot of will power and determination to do this correctly.

EMPLOYED

Very few driving schools employ driving instructors. A couple do while on a trainee licence, but it's rare and complicated. A driving school would supply the car and you would pay tax as an employed person. The driving school would probably need to charge pupils VAT on the lessons, whereas they do not for self-employed instructors.

INDEPENDENT OR FRANCHISED?

This is a big question and one that is not answered easily. Often, it's down to personal choice but there are a lot of independent instructors out there, who are independent because they feel they were with a bad franchise. Sometimes this is true and sometimes it was the instructors' expectations. There are many independent instructors who should be with a 'good' franchise. If they were, they would not be going bust. There are many driving instructors who have been successful as an independent instructor for years and will remain to do so. There are many, quoted as 4 out of 5, who will give up within two years. They leave a franchise with a full diary, manage to maintain it for a year or two, then find it all falls apart. They need to do some proper marketing but it's too little too late. Currently, post COVID, every driving school is busy. Many schools are enjoying this but are not thinking about when this surplus pupil supply runs out. It will and then we will see many struggles. Currently they think they are successful, and they are, but more by accident than skill. If you are the sort of person who is good at marketing, then this might be the challenge you are looking for. There are added problems, like, who will answer the phone? It's a criminal offence for you to do it while teaching or driving. Pupils rarely leave voicemails and if they do, you'll struggle to call them back. Maybe you have a partner at home who could do this? Maybe you could use a professional call answering service? There are options. I set up my school to help those GOOD instructors who were good at the teaching but found the business side hard. Instructors who might not be instructors if they had not chosen to work for a franchise. I like to call it a 'done for you service'. We do everything that a professional instructor would do for themselves, but they don't have the time. Things like, pupils licence checks, booking tests for pupils, pupil packs, and answering those long difficult questions on the phone and a lot more. Yes, a franchise costs money but saves a lot of work. It's a choice only you can make. I support and help a lot of independent instructors too; they are good at their business but still need that support occasionally.

DIFFERENT TYPES OF FRANCHISE

This section would not be complete without explaining some different types of franchise.

THE BIG NATIONAL DRIVING SCHOOL

There are a few national driving schools. Generally, they tend to be the highest price, but you are working with a national brand. You can tell me their names as they are so widely known. They do not always have the highest lesson prices though. Often, you are just a number and can be one of many driving instructors in an area. I worked for a national company for seven years while I increased my qualifications. I became a fleet qualified instructor and an instructor trainer with them. I tended to work from my own recommendations, but occasionally would need top ups from them. Some instructors have worked for these driving schools for many years and find it suits them well.

THE MEDIUM SIZED OR REGIONAL DRIVING SCHOOLS

There are some very good medium sized driving schools and some not so good. Some are looking to make it into the national category and the only way they can do this, is to get as many instructors as they can. I used to work for one of these too. Each month would see 10-15 new instructors join and each month you'd see 12-17 instructors leave. I related it to a bucket with no bottom and while they were topping up the bucket and celebrating, nobody was sealing the hole at the bottom. There are good ones who recruit instructors to meet demands or expected demands of pupils. I know with my school, exactly how many instructors I can feed with enough pupils in each area. I know that if I set up in a new area, I can get a page in the first three positions of Google in about a month, sometimes much quicker. I know I can use many different paid for marketing options too. I know not to take on too many instructors.

THE SMALL DRIVING SCHOOLS.

There are many of these, I'm not referring to the independent instructor, the one-person-band, but driving schools taking on an additional instructor or two. Some of these have found that in good times, they have too many pupils so recruit an instructor to cover the overload. But what happens when the work goes low? The owner is normally working as an instructor themselves so who answers the phone, does the marketing etc? Building a driving school takes a lot of effort and requires a good team behind you.

THE SOLO INSTRUCTOR

This can be great if you live in a small village and everyone gets to know you, or if you have one of those personalities that shines out and the recommendations just keep flowing.

CONTRACT OR NO CONTRACT

A much-debated point on social media, contract, or no contract. Well, a good contract will support you as well as the driving school. It can tell you what the driving school will do for you and lay this down in a contract. You will know what to expect as a driving school is not likely to put something they can't offer. It might specify a minimum period. Setting up a new instructor properly takes time and money, and a driving school will want some minimum time to recoup this. Where this goes wrong is when the school does not provide the service and the instructor can't get out of it. Then contracts get a bad name. Check to see what the school is offering you. I write in a minimum pupil amount I will guarantee to give, If I did not honour this, you could get out of your contract. Often schools say they don't use a contract, this is often because they do not want to promise you anything. It sounds good at first but if they supply no pupils, you won't pay the bills so a contract that ensures you're protected is better. A contract must work both ways.

SUMMARY

There are many choices when becoming a driving instructor. As a good driving instructor, you need to concentrate on your teaching first and foremost. If you think you can do this, and run the marketing and business side, then independent could be right for you. Never be afraid if it did not work out, going back to a franchise if needed. Don't give up, especially if you are a good instructor because this profession needs you badly.

CHAPTER 5: YOUR BUSINESS ROLE

Professionalism

What it takes to be a 'good' instructor

I am often asked, 'is there a good living to be made as a Driving Instructor?' The simple answer is YES. However, it will not come to you. Now you are a self-employed person responsible for your own success and demise! My answer is always followed with 'there is if you exceed your pupil's demands.' What do I mean? Look at the test centre, a popular place where you will see Driving Instructors gathered. Many are very scruffy, and cars look like they could do with a wash. There are many unprofessional things you will see, all you must do is 'stand out from the crowd' and from the evidence often seen, you don't have to do too much. You are a professional so start your career by looking and acting professional. I dress for work; it would be all too easy to think my pupils would not care what I look like and for many, they don't. Think of the wider implications, what if mum or dad saw you through the window, what would their impression be? They won't have the advantage of your pupil who falls in love with your wonderful persona! Meet the demands of your pupil; sounds simple but is often overlooked. It was Margret Thatcher (sorry guys) who said, '*do not bring me problems, bring me solutions.*' Look at how you can meet these pupils' needs and you will be on to a winner. You have entered a service industry where you are on show all the time. What you say and do can make or break you so always give yourself the advantage and choose your words carefully. An innocent joke can end up being misread. Avoid over familiarities such as 'love' and 'darling' save these for your loves and darlings. People do find this creepy despite what you may think. If you go to any continuing professional development event, look at the successful instructors and see what they all have in common.

KEEPING A PROFESSIONAL DISTANCE

Keeping a professional distance is not just a physical thing but an emotional one too. Yes, you need to ensure you don't invade the pupils' physical space apart from those occasional times you might need to grab the steering wheel. But its more than that. Some instructors get too involved personally with their pupils, some way too involved, but it's important to keep the relationship professional. Start by looking professional, an aspect covered later. You are your pupils' teacher and as such you need to **keep that relationship professional.**

It's unfortunate that we hear in the media from time to time about how a driving instructor has crossed that line. It's all too easy to start to be the pupil's friend and go and meet them at football matches or at work for example. **Think about how this could be construed**, what somebody else might think. I am not saying do not care or take an interest, far from it but don't cross that line thinking they are your confidant. I hear too often about instructors who would share their personal worries and complaints with pupils. Many discuss other pupils with pupils having a 'laugh' at them.

- Never discuss other pupils. It may seem ok to have a laugh or talk about that strange pupil, but all they think is *"what do they say about **me** to the other pupils?"*

Sometimes a pupil may want to confide in you, and that's ok, but **save it until after the lesson.** What may seem like a joke or just harmless fun can *and will* backfire on you, sometimes with disastrous consequences. Over the years there have been countless stories that have occurred in driving lessons (from other schools) and that are truly beyond belief.

PUPIL RAPPORT

Probably one of the most essential (and I should say obvious) skills for a driving instructor is that of gaining rapport with your pupil. **To be fair, it's the same for any business really.**

So, why is it so important to gain rapport with your pupil? I'd like to think this was a rhetorical question but for the benefit of the doubt I'm going to explain.

Rapport, so what? Does it really help make safe drivers?

As driving instructors, we are teaching a life skill, a skill that will give some a future, most independence and many a way of enjoyment. Part of our role, as defined by the DVSA, is to encourage our pupils to evaluate their beliefs, attitudes, and values in driving.

Without rapport, coaching will not happen. Lessons will be one sided with you talking and the pupil grunting, shrugging shoulders, or replying continually with 'I don't know' at best.

This helps them to look at and manage risks associated with not only skills to drive safely, but trip related influences and motives. Two examples of this are: 'Can I drive while under the influence of alcohol?' or 'I'm really tired after this 12-hour shift, should I be driving?'

It's great to get paid for our job, but its nicer to love our job and get paid for it.

There's the teaching side, and then of course there's the business side of our role. Pupils just do not want to sit in a car with someone they do not have rapport with. They will cancel lessons (we've heard a lot of instructors complaining about this recently). Pupils will be negative and passive in their driving lessons, or sometimes even stroppy or uncommunicative. This is not good for business - after all, we're all looking to get paid.

So, let's look at some tips to building rapport.

ASK QUESTIONS.

On that first meeting be curious and ask questions likely to create conversations but avoid topics like family and pets unless they bring them up themselves. While most people will wax lyrical about their family and pets, for a few it's a way to shut them down.

Once they've raised a subject then it's good grounds for the future. A great opening line to a new pupil can be "Tell me about yourself." They will mention things of value to you. Ask about their motivations for learning to drive and their aspirations when they have passed. This is so valuable in the weeks ahead during driving lessons. They can be used as encouragement and in a supportive role. You can use this as ways to enhance driving lessons.

Something you may not know about me is that I am also a qualified teacher of English as a foreign language, in teaching foreign languages, we use these skills a lot to develop our students. It might be business English they need help with, so we use real examples of English from their business. We are helping them not just to learn the language but learn the language they will use. This equally applies to driving. If they want to learn to drive to go to work, take them from home to work and back. This gives real purpose to their learning.

WHAT ARE YOU HEARING?

Listen to what they have to say, even if someone's views do not match your own, they are still valuable views. The world would be a boring place if we all wore pink, even as bright as the colour can be. Listen to your pupils throughout lessons and hear what they are saying. A normally placid pupil who would not normally say boo to a goose but says 'I am shitting myself at this roundabout' is saying more than "This roundabout is difficult." Oh! And don't have this conversation on the roundabout either.

Try to use empathy where you can. Many driving instructors talk about how they hate their Part Three exam or Standards Test but fail to see the connection and empathy in their pupils sitting the driving test. So, listen to what they say and offer connections to how they feel.

OPEN UP (A LITTLE)

A little honesty can go a long way, tell them something about yourself that they can associate with. They will feel they can trust you and are more likely to be open with you. But on this note be careful what you tell them. A year or so ago an associate school of mine had a complaint from a parent that the instructor was telling her daughter about his marriage problems. He went into very specific details. It was clear that although the learner must have appeared to be joining in with the conversation, I suspect body language was not 'joining in.' The daughter proudly told her mum how unfortunate her driving instructor was and about his marital problems. They were not impressed he was discussing this with her.

You do need to remember who you are talking to. Keep your conversations strictly professional and avoid conversation on sex, religion, and politics at all costs.

MIRROR THEM

According to Mindtools, a great way to gain rapport is to subtly mirror your pupils. Match their body language and stance (position). You can even try to match their breathing rate, but a great one I find is to match their energy level. Energy is after all what makes the world go around, and if you're a particularly high-energy person then you won't like sitting with a low-energy person and vice versa.

WHAT YOU WEAR DOES COUNT!

I have talked about what you wear before on a business front but it's equally important from a teaching or rather coaching point of view. First impressions do count. It's a fact that people judge you in the first few seconds. Pupils must feel comfortable sitting next to you. I've seen instructors who try to dress like their pupils (yes, a 58-year-old man with a baseball cap on sideways looks like a ****.)

I've seen instructors dressing like they are trying to impress their pupils rather than teach them. In our role, rapport is about dressing just a little better than our pupils. As a fleet trainer, I would always wear my suit. When I turned up for a client I never knew if I was going to be taking the managing director out or the storeman. If I turned up and I needed to dress down, I would make an excuse to retrieve something from my car and remove the jacket.

We need to look smart and professional. Those who follow me know it's no secret how I always used to wear a shirt and tie when delivering driving lessons. This worked so well for me, as I attracted more influential pupils, and my lesson rates went up. You don't necessarily need to wear a tie, but you need to be better dressed than your pupils. A joke at the test centre I once heard.

> "How do you tell the pupils from the driving instructors at the test centre?
>
> The pupils are the better dressed ones."

It was so true.

DRESS FOR WORK

It is a fact of life that people do judge on appearances. Think how you expect a bank manager to look like or a manager. Does the supervisor look any different than the workforce? How would you expect a driving instructor to dress? I've seen all sorts. From those shiny black string vests, tiny shorts leaving little to the imagination and flip flops. I've seen shell suits, jeans that look like someone was working on a farm and shoes with holes in them.

You're a professional driving instructor – so you should look like one. In our industry, too many instructors come to lessons looking very scruffy. This gives a bad image of you as an instructor as well as a driving school. You don't need to wear a shirt and tie like I used to, but dress appropriately. How often I see very scruffy driving instructors in the driving test centre. It is something remarked upon by examiners sometimes.

Remember, mum and dad will probably be peeking behind the curtains as you pull up for the driving lessons. Or dad is conveniently washing the car or in the front garden when you return. Get out and say hello and have a short chat if you can. Those of you that do will know the conversation will usually turn to 'I could not do your job' or 'is it right that they don't have to use every gear now or indicate when moving off sometimes'. This is your chance to gain some valuable empathy. It's how I ended up with so many recommendations.

Now I know that many driving instructors reading the above will totally disagree with me. They will say you can wear what you want. Remember, this book is not about how to become a driving instructor but how to become a GOOD driving instructor. How to set yourself apart from the many who feel 'average is good enough'. How to stand out with not just your pupils, but their parents and other establishments like schools. It worked for me and it can work for you.

A SMELLY PROBLEM

Now you'd have thought that in today's world we would not need to talk about personal hygiene, but it comes up all too often. A common complaint from pupils is how bad their instructor smelt. Some time ago while delivering a training course for new instructors in what was a rather small classroom, I was instantly drawn to the most horrendous smell. I mean not just a little whiffy, but something that made my stomach churn. I mean so bad, I thought maybe someone had soiled themselves. My co-presenter was clearly having trouble and started to spray herself with perfume. We were exchanging glances of horror and as I moved towards her the smell was coming from a client her side. We opened windows and there were noses twitching all around from other course members.

During a tea break it was clear who the offender was and my bosses at the time were arguing about who was going to confront them. Heck, I volunteered! Not an easy task, but I went outside for a chat with him and had already put a can of deodorant in my pocket that I carried just in case and told him there had been complaints. He told me he had been getting complaints from his pupils too. I had occasion to speak with an examiner about something and the examiner also commented about complaints from other examiners on his part three test...yet he still did nothing. **He didn't see it as his problem.** The mind boggles!"

This can be an embarrassing situation for a pupil, and they will often make excuses to cancel future lessons instead of broaching the subject. The smell of cigarette smoke can have an adverse effect on many pupils too. Some just do not like it. Instructors are often not aware about how bad it is. Getting lots of annoying cancellations? Make sure you're presented well before blaming the pupil.

YOUR USE OF LANGUAGE

The language you use with your pupils is very important. Not just swearing but discrimination. Often words and expressions may be used quite innocently, but your pupils (especially the younger ones) may feel uncomfortable. Even when pupils use bad language, you are the professional and should refrain. What image are you trying to give?

Be sure to avoid swearing in a professional environment and while delivering driving lessons. Avoid stereotypes too, 'white van man' or 'typical BMW driver' are just two I hear a lot. Bear in mind that one of the competencies on the part three and Standards Check is 'did the trainer maintain an appropriate and non-discriminatory language'. This needs to extend to outside of lessons too if in an encounter with the public.

Sometimes it may be easy to forget that the badge on your polo shirt or the roof box on top of your car are still there at the end of the day when lessons finish. It's vitally important to uphold the standards you set as a driving instructor while still representing yourself as one. Always remain professional, as one of the most common complaints from pupils in the industry is that of inappropriate language or inappropriate behaviour.

BEING PUNCTUAL

This may sound basic but often driving schools get calls asking, *"where's my driving instructor?"*

If you're not sure where the house is, look it up before. Never assume. It's always better to arrive early, suss out the location and wait around the corner. Don't turn up too early either. Pupils are nervous and turning up early puts them in a panic, making them feel like they need to apologise for not being ready or prepared.

Occasionally things happen that mean you're going to be late, so stop, call the pupil, and let them know what's happening.

We all know ourselves that there's nothing worse than waiting for someone and wondering *"Are they coming? Are they late? Have I got the wrong time?"* It all adds to the nerves. I see this a lot, instructors start to get sloppy, a few minutes here and there but it adds up.

WHAT YOU PUT ON SOCIAL MEDIA COUNTS

When making comments on social media remember it's in the public domain. Even closed groups are monitored and you never know who's in them. It never ceases to amaze me the number of offensive comments made by instructors or the 'I told my shite pupil' sort of comments that appear daily in forums. Yes, examiners read these forums too.

Pupils read social media, their parents read social media and the DVSA read social media. Why do so many instructors use insulting and derogatory comments about pupils. Calling them "numpties," "wastes of space" and sometimes far worse. I must ask myself, "what is the rapport like with their pupils?"

In summary, building a rapport with your pupils is easy when you start it right. It's no more than polite conversation. I am always so jealous of my wife how she instantly gains rapport with people and makes friends so easily. Her secret is a genuine desire to be interested about them, and this can go a long way in driving instruction.

MARKETING

MAKE IT KNOWN
YOU HAVE ARRIVED.

So now you're a driving instructor, a self-employed businessperson. Now it's time to let everyone know you've arrived. Start by telling friends and family, but don't fall foul of offering them too much discount! **You want them to come to you because they trust YOU** and not because you're cheap. This is a mistake many novice instructors make, feeling they owe the family or friends, and it helps with start-up.

Friends and family can be a great source of introductions to help kick-start your business as **everybody likes to recommend someone they know.** Your driving school should supply you with business cards that you can hand out to people you know and keep a supply in your car. At the very least, you want a 5-star review from your friend or relative as a pupil.

Look for every opportunity to tell people about yourself. A very common mistake is to be shy about not telling people. Do you have teenage children in the family? If you have a part time job while you're training, then what opportunities can this bring for spreading the word?

The truth is that we'll provide you with all the pupils you'll need. But you'll also naturally get recommendations in the local area, and this is a great way to build your reputation as a driving instructor. I was doing training with someone who was complaining he never had enough pupils. He had very large magnetic stickers he had created from the stickers his driving school supplied. I asked him why he had magnetic stickers and he said, 'I don't want nobody knowing I am a driving instructor when I finish work, so I take them off'. He also wanted to finish his training early because he was a football coach to 17-year-olds. I could not understand why he would not let them know he was an instructor.

RECOMMENDATIONS

Whilst in business we say, 'recommendations are not a form of marketing', it is still good to get them as it shows you are doing your job right. Never build a business on recommendations alone, it will come unstuck one day. Recommendations are a sign that your pupils like you. You must be doing things right to get recommendations. For every first time pass you get, you will receive four times as many recommendations as from other passes. But why is it that some instructors rarely get recommendations? One of the main reasons is they do not ask for them. There are two best times to ask. One on those first lessons, they are excited and should have moved the car for the first time. This type of excitement is infectious, and this cascaded out to their friends and family. At this time, they will be open to being asked as they will want their friends to share what they are feeling. The second is when they have passed their test. Again, they are happy and will want to share this.

Do not be afraid to ask for recommendations. Some instructors offer incentives like, if they recommend a friend then when the friend has had five lessons then they will get a free lesson or a voucher for something. Personally, I don't like this practice as it defeats the point of a recommendation.

A note on recommendations.

It is not wise to think recommendations will always keep coming. There is a 2-year cycle of friends, and you can be the best instructor in the world, and they might stop coming. No business should ever rely on one source of marketing.

TARGET YOUR ADVERTISING

Putting out leaflets and advertising can be costly and is sometimes a hit and miss approach. Doing it correctly though, can bring in pupils and the right types of pupils and can give the independent driving instructor a market that the franchises who have the top positions in Google, will not be doing. Ask yourself 'where are the learners like who I want to teach?' There is little point in doing a leaflet campaign to bungalows lived in by the elderly. Whilst you might pick up the odd pupil here, the time and effort are not always worth it unless you do it correctly. Start in one area, usually looking for the three and four bedroomed properties and distribute your leaflets. Then look at this area and see what shops offer postcard adverts and put your postcards in these shops. Use these shops if you need a bottle of water or anything and if you need to park in between lessons and have a sandwich etc. then do this in the same area. Try to drive through the same area during lessons as much as possible too. Four weeks later go back and deliver more leaflets to the same houses and the same again in four more weeks. What you are now doing is saturating your area and getting maximum presence. Advertising specialists will tell you that you need to touch your customers many times before they buy. This multi-approach can reap you customers just like the pizza advert we see come through the door. True, we put them in the bin, but when we need a pizza where do we go!? Do the same again in another area once you have picked up some pupils from the first. Too many independent driving instructors sit at home when they have no pupils, just waiting for the phone to ring. If you are not being pro-active about pupil generation, it can be a long wait.

Where do you go for your breaks? I used to use the café opposite the college where the 17-year-olds would be. Again, this got my car noticed and many times pupils would come and ask me how much my lessons were. I would offer a discounted or even free lesson there and then. My pupils also knew where I was and would often bring their friends for help with the theory or booking of their test and guess how many started having lessons!

OFFERS

Offers are a fact of life in many forms of business. If you want your pupils to choose you from your advert, then you need to stand out. If the pupil already knows you then in theory, it is a done deal but what if they do not and you are putting out an advert. Yes, if they are looking for a specific type of lesson and you have a niche market then you might be ok but for the run of the mill pupil, you will often need an offer. It's no good thinking 'I have this advanced driving qualification or that skill', pupils assume all instructors have them and it means nothing to them. When you get them in the car, and give them their first lesson, then is the time to show why YOU should be their instructor.

Now don't run away thinking I am promoting 10 hours for £99.00 or anything like that, although these offers can have a place. For example, if you are trying to build a diary quickly and get some Social Media testimonials to build the business. The best offer is a short-term offer designed to get the pupil who does not know you into the driving seat. These will be the pupils who have not had anyone recommended by their friends or family and quite frankly do not know who to choose. If they did, they would not be trawling the internet. These pupils, you have one hit to make them book online or call you and you need a catchy little offer or deal for them. Open Google and look at the driving schools there, what driving school would you chose?

It is a great idea to theme your offers. Christmas special or weekend deals for example can work quite well. I have always been a fan of the first 2 hours for £40 or even £30. This is a very short-term offer that gives you a pupil and little commitment for your pupil. Often pupils do not want long term deals in case they do not like the instructor and must sit with them for 10 or more hours.

I am just skimming the surface with offers. There are many good marketing books on this. All I am doing here is saying, offers are needed from time to time. If you are marketing from Google or Facebook, you need to stand out. Saying you are the best driving instructor in the world cuts no ice. Get them in the car with an offer, then show them you are the best driving instructor in the world.

Of course, if you are with a franchise then they will do all the above for you and supply you with pupils. This is what the franchise model is all about. They should use many different types of marketing and usually occupy one of the top 3 Google positions for the areas that you cover.

Offers are often criticised for being a cheap lesson and often I hear comments 'how can a driving instructor make a living on £5, or £9.99 an hour etc? well they're not!

Let us look at some examples currently on offer from schools.

Example one

10 lessons for £199 normal rate £30 per hour

Pupil needs 34 hours, 10 at £199 + 24 at £30/hour income = £919 adjustment for offer means lesson rate is £27.02 per hour. This is not a good offer in today's climate.

Example three

First 2 hours for £30 normal rate £30 per hour

Pupil needs 34 hours, 2 at £30 + 32 at £30 income = £990 adjustment for offer means lesson rate is £29.12 per hour, that's not too bad.

N.B The example used was from a very old marketing and

would need adjusting today. It is worth noting that currently, every driving instructor is busy due to the huge demand for driving lessons after the COVID. This will not continue forever, and marketing will be needed when the number of pupils calms down.

Offers are something you can turn on and off. Just like the supermarket or any one of the high Street retailers. Yes, there are instructors who say they never do offers, and you might find you don't need to, but it depends where your marketplace is. If you are Bob the local village instructor, you're unlikely to ever need an offer. Pupils will come to you because you're Bob and you teach everyone in the village. Pupils do not generally worry about price, because everyone was taught by Bob and knows him. If you live in a big city or town and you are marketing on a website or a social media platform, you might need an offer to compete with the other offers. Pupils here do not know you and will buy on price. Once you have given them the offer lesson/s and shown them how good you are and you can give them what they want, freedom on the road, they will not think too much about the price. Providing you are not too unreasonable.

GIFT VOUCHERS

Gift vouchers can be a great way of promoting your business, especially around Christmas etc. Producing a nice-looking voucher to give to parents and pupils can be nice and something tangible to use. However, they will not work IF you do not tell people about them. Display them on your website ahead of Christmas and use a campaign to tell people what you are doing. This is where leaflets can help too, by giving them to pupils and distributing them to publicise the vouchers. I would not necessarily drop the price for the vouchers but would offer something extra like a free Highway Code or other book, be imaginative. I once knew an instructor who offered a free pot of marmalade, yes marmalade!!! It was so unusual that parents loved it and it was something he made himself. I often like to look in magazines for the adverts to see how original some are and how I can use them for my school.

BIRTHDAY SURPRISES

Many people are looking to buy lessons as birthday or similar gifts, especially if bought in conjunction with the gift vouchers. It will be important that if this is the case then you do not call the pupil before the lesson, however, get the contact number of someone else who will confirm the lesson and that the pupil has their licence etc. I would certainly look forward to taking a photo with the permission of the pupils on this first lesson and this could be given to them as part of the memory.

PASS PLUS

Pass Plus, while not as popular as it was once, is still just about in existence. To deliver Pass Plus, all you need is to be a qualified ADI. Your first, and subsequent, Pass Plus packs can be obtained by logging on to your Integrated Register of Driver Trainers (IRDT) site, explained later, or by calling the DSA Pass Plus unit. Pass Plus is a road safety initiative started in November 1995.

The Pass Plus scheme was introduced to help newly qualified young drivers gain valuable driving experience and reduce the risk of them being involved in an accident. It is a structured syllabus that must be adhered to for the insurance discounts to be given. It is a good idea to tell your pupils about Pass Plus right from the start. Talk to them throughout their lessons mentioning what you will cover when they pass and how Pass Plus can help. Many instructors fail at the first hurdle by never really mentioning it until the pupil passes. Pass Plus is a minimum of six hours and covers such things as motorways, adverse weather, and night driving to name a few. It can be done over one day or split into smaller bites. It is up to what your pupil wants. On completion you fill in a form that is sent to the DSA who sends the pupil a certificate.

THINGS THAT CAN GO WRONG.

CANCELLED LESSONS

One of the most common problems facing Driving Instructors is cancellations. The forums are awash with 'advice' on how to handle them. Normally this advice is very negative in the form of 'bin em' or 'always charge them'. It is a fact of life that you will get these no matter how professional you are or what safeguards you take. Like a pub landlord who has ullage, a shop keeper who has petty theft and the baker who throws good cake away at the end of the day. You will have to accept this as part of your profession. Do not let cancellations get you down or worried. Build them into your working model and budget for them. Cancellations can account for around two lessons a week. However, that is not to say we cannot try to reduce them.

I believe many cancelations are due to the pupil not wanting to have the lesson. I mean, they are not enjoying the driving lesson for one reason or another and will look to cancel for any reason they can. Your pupils need to enjoy their driving lessons and not think they are a chore.

If you are not with a driving school that does this for you, texting pupils the night before a lesson can often remind them. Use a simple text template that says something like;

> *This is to remind you of your Driving lesson tomorrow, at xxxx time. If there are any problems, please text me back.*

Ensuring you always turn up and on time will set the standard too. Fill in a pupil's record card with the next date of the lesson too.

REGULAR TIME
AND DAYS

I used to find a regular slot that fits in with almost every pupil's other activities, so they have the same time and day every week just like their college lessons. I used to do this after the first driving lesson, finding out what regular timeslot would work best for the pupil. Sometimes their best time slot was already taken, so we would find the next best compromise, but I would make a note of this so that when that slot did become available, I could offer it to them.

How you handle the actual cancellations can really make or break your future as a Driving Instructor.

When they cancel, and they will, do not immediately charge them. This shows a very uncaring nature. Ring them the night after and show concern, ask them if they are ok. Show regret by saying 'I am sorry I missed you, is everything ok?' They will explain the reason. Sometimes valid, sometimes foolish, however the important thing is to get them back in the car next lesson. Simply re-arrange the next lesson and ensure you send a text to confirm. Now this might seem a little too 'friendly' but this is a calculated business move. On that next lesson mention nothing until after the lesson. Say how you are enjoying teaching them and here is where you can politely remind them of any cancellation clause and inform them next time you will have to charge them. Nine out of ten times there will be no other problems.

Let's see how this works.

Scenario one

Pupils cancel on lesson 10 so you ring them up and say they will have to pay double next week. The likelihood of the pupil showing up for that next lesson is slim.

Outcome one

You will lose payment for lesson 10 and all the subsequent 40 lessons.

Scenario two

Pupil cancels on lesson 10; you ring up and show concern then book in lesson 11. They will most probably show.

Outcome two

Lost payment for lesson 10 but will get payment for the subsequent 40 lessons, in fact you will still get the payment for lesson 10 as they will still need that lesson sometime!

I would go so far as to say how you handle your cancellations can increase your business, as instructors who handle their cancellations fairly but firmly will attract pupils. You must look at the bigger picture when handling cancellations not just at the immediate lesson. Again, I reiterate, this is not being soft or easy, if the cancellations start to become a habit, then these needs addressing. Firstly, I would ascertain what the problem is. Do they look like they are enjoying the lessons? There might be problems at home/college. If you have the right rapport, then some simple questions can be used to find out why. I've had them. The pupil who was telling his parents he was having driving lessons, whilst all the time he was at home with his girlfriend. One guy, it turned out his parents wanted him to drive so he could ferry his sister to school etc. He did not want to learn to drive. Another, when it came to mum having to stump up for more lessons because he had not turned up for so many, she, a doctor, argued with me how her son would 'never miss a driving lesson'. She called me back two days later to apologise, apparently, he'd got addicted to drugs. She booked him into a rehab clinic, he came back and was the most reliable pupil ever.

CHRISTMAS CANCELLATIONS

A note on the most cancelled lessons of the year, Christmas.

The first year I worked as an instructor, I worked over Christmas, well when I say I worked I mean I was available. All my pupils were asking me 'am I working over Christmas?' as they said they would all like lessons. Each morning I would get up, shower and dress only to find one by one my pupils were cancelling, sore throats, sick children and even dogs were amongst the excuses. One day I had 4 lessons and already 3 had cancelled. When the 4th called and before she had chance to say anything, I was quick to tell her if she wanted to cancel too then go ahead, I was a little short and suddenly felt very guilty as she asked, 'was I working' as she really wanted her lesson. I apologised and said of course I would be there, and I did the lesson and did not have the heart to charge her, sorry Leanne if you ever read this.

Now at the time of writing this, as I have explained there are more pupils than driving instructors can deal with. It is becoming common place to just get rid of a pupil for any reason and replace them. This might seem the easiest option, but I want you to consider, is it the best option long term? Could this have a negative impact on your school later? One day, the pupil lesson demand will return to normal, and I see the amount of driving instructors is increasing. So be careful here and think right.

BREAKDOWNS

When I say breakdowns, I refer to the car not the driving instructor. Breakdowns can happen at the most inconvenient times (is there ever a convenient time?) and are sometimes unavoidable; however, there are steps you can take to avoid them or at least limit the consequences. Having your car regularly serviced is, I would have thought, obvious, but do not forget those daily and weekly checks. As a safety net I always used to do every 'show me, tell me check', with the pupil as I picked them up for their driving test. That way if something did blow on the way to a driving test the pupil knew it was ok before. It also gives you a chance to fix anything at the last minute, this was on top of my usual morning walk around the car before lessons. It is surprising how many cars are refused on tests because of simple faults like bulbs blown or nails in tyres, all of which must have happened on the way to the test centre according to the instructor! In a post recently, I saw an instructor complaining that the examiner was refusing to take his car on a test because it had a 4cm cut in it. I found it difficult to believe this would have happened 'en route'. But I was more concerned how instructors thought that the attitude of the examiner was being unreasonable. It is not uncommon for instructors to advise sticking chewing gum or blue tac in the cut and painting over it or turning the tyre around so the examiner can't see it. The mind boggles as to why they are in a profession that is supposed to be about road safety.

A good idea is to carry spare bulbs (kits can be bought for each vehicle relatively cheaply). Also ensure you have any tools needed to change the bulb as some vehicles have special fixings. Practice changing the bulbs in case it happens to you on test as the examiner will give you a couple of minutes to sort it out. It is impossible to change bulbs quickly on some vehicles, so find out if yours is one of them. Spare fuses are a good idea too; fuses can often be blown when changing a bulb. Disposable gloves to keep your hands clean and some cleaning rags can be useful as well.

Never try to cover up information lights on the dashboard, this has been tried before and the examiners are wise to it. If the information light is glowing, then have it checked out. I heard of one example where the instructor covered the airbag warning light with a postage stamp!

Carry spare bulbs, kits can be bought for each vehicle relatively cheaply.

USEFUL TIPS

ROOF BOXES

Did you know that there is a right and wrong way for the top box to be positioned on your car? The "L" part should be placed over the driver's side.

It is amazing how often you will see dirty roof boxes on cars. Given that this is a form of advertising, what does it say about your driving school? Give your roof box a good wash in soapy water from time to time. Ensure if it is frosty, you wipe the roof over first otherwise the roof box may not stay on. In normal conditions a roof box should stay on at speeds of 140mph; that's 70mph driving into a 70mph headwind in case you were thinking of driving at 140mph!

TIPS TO HELP CREATE A CALM ATMOSPHERE

Bring two cotton balls. Place a drop of Essence of Lavender oil on each and pop them in the side door pocket next to the driver's seat. On hot days it will keep you calm without making you feel drowsy.

For nervous pupils, especially on the day of the test, there are several herbal remedies such as "Calms" tablets or "Bach's Rescue Remedy" that may be useful to your pupils. Do not keep them or administer them yourself though, just advise your pupils as appropriate!

www.maps.google.com

As a driving school, we often get phone calls from pupils, 10 minutes after their first lesson should have started, asking where the instructor is. When we get hold of the instructor, they say they are looking for the house. This is not giving a good first impression. I will talk about soon, the introduction call. Calling the pupils when you first get them to introduce yourself. Confirm on the call where you will pick them up and if there are any difficulties. Make sure you know where the pickup point is even if you must go early and wait round the corner.

If you haven't already come across this website and you don't use a satnav, you may find it very useful for finding pupil addresses – you only need to key in the postcode. This site is very useful for setting up your training ground and routes for pupils in the early days. The 'Google Earth' or 'Satellite' view enables you to look at the layouts and types of junctions.

YOUR MOBILE PHONE MESSAGE

So many times, I call instructors and get 'this is the O2 answer phone service. How do I know I've called the correct person? Can I leave sensitive details on this answerphone, like the phone number and address of a 17-year-old pupil? Under the data protection act we all have a duty to ensure that information given out is going to the correct person. To ensure that messages are left on the correct person's voice mail you should ensure you have recorded a professional message on your answerphone. This is probably going to be your pupil's first contact with you. Your message should say something like the following.

> *"Hello this is Fred Smith from 'your school name'*
> *Sorry I cannot take your call right now as I am on a lesson*
> *If you leave your name and number, I will get straight back to you as soon as I can; thank you for calling."*

Some of you might like to omit your surname if you are worried about unsolicited contact later. For this reason, we have omitted the surnames of female members of staff in our office.

The all-important introduction call

When a driving school franchise sends you a new pupil, it is a good idea to call, not text, that pupil personally and introduce yourself. You might find a quick text giving your name and who you are so they can store the number, is wise first. Pupils often ignore calls from numbers they don't know. This is so important. As a driving school ourselves and looking after many other driving schools, we have found that the driving instructors who do not call their pupils to introduce themselves, get a huge number of no shows on the first driving lesson. Pupils are nervous for their first driving lesson and if the instructor calls, it really helps them start to know them and ease the pressure. When you do speak with your pupil, make sure you sound friendly and take an interest. Find out a little about them first before booking the lesson and develop a rapport. Ensure they have their provisional licence and remind them to bring it with them on the first lesson. Book in their lesson as soon as you can, keep the motivation. Once you have booked the lesson let them know how much you are looking forward to the lesson and confirm the date and time. Always remind them to bring their glasses if they wear them and to wear "sensible footwear". This has happened a few times, but I will always remember one time. A trainee instructor who had traveled some distance for training with me, got in the car wearing flip flops. We were doing the part two training where she would be driving. I asked her about the footwear and asked, 'what did the Highway Code say'? She replied, not flip flops. Well, it talks of appropriate footwear, but I accepted her answer. She then explained that she was thinking that morning before driving to me, whether flip flops would be appropriate. So, on that basis, you'd have thought she had brought another pair of shoes, even as spares just in case but, no, she had not. In my early days as an instructor, against my better judgement I allowed a girl to drive in flip flops. She had to brake sharply, and her foot slid through the flip flop catching the steering column where she cut her toe. I had to use the dual brake that depressed her brake almost trapping her foot. NEVER AGAIN WOULD I ALLOW FLIP FLOPS. I guarantee that pupil has never worn them driving again.

TEXTING YOUR PUPILS

Once you've delivered your first lessons, it is a good idea to establish the best way to communicate with each pupil. Most pupils are happy with texting and it's a great way of communicating as if needed, it leaves an evidence trail of messages date stamped. Most franchises will have some form of automated text message service for reminding pupils of future and upcoming lessons, if you're not with a franchise, then maybe it's a case of sitting down in the evening and sending a quick text reminder. You can set up templates for this to make it easier. Typical reminders would be before every lesson, maybe 24 or 48 hours before. (We use 48 hours before)

It is a good idea when you first meet them to get them to put your preferred contact number into their phone's memory and their number into your phone too. Pupils will sometimes ignore messages from numbers they do not recognise. I once sent a message to a young married lady who had previously asked me to let her know if I had any extra lessons spare due to her fourth coming driving test. I said, '*I may have a cancellation next Wednesday as a pupil was ill and would let her know.*' On the Tuesday, having text the pupil who I thought would cancel, I learned she was better and could have her lesson. My response to the first pupil went like this;

'*Hi, I can't see you Wednesday but will see you Saturday as usual.*'

Her husband picked up the message and she had no idea who

had sent it as she had not saved my number. He demanded to know who she was meeting as she always went out at the weekend with her 'sister' and I think he was a little suspicious (or insecure). She could not work out who it was from. It was not until she got in my car for the usual Saturday morning lesson, I noticed she seemed upset, enquiring about her state she explained how she had a strange text message, and her husband was going mad. I then explained it was me and it all made sense to her then although I'm still don't believe the husband was convinced. I was nearly cited in the divorce proceeding. Please get the pupil to put your number in their phone, it might save a lot of hassle later.

ACCOUNTS

It is easy as a driving instructor to get behind on the paperwork. Putting it off for a rainy day, but it soon mounts up. Decide from the beginning how you will do your accounts and keep records. There is nothing too complicated about driving instructor accounts but if you are not sure then use an accountant. Their services can range from everything like filling in the monthly accounts to final submission with HMRC or just the final submission and you do the monthly or weekly bookkeeping. The HMRC themselves run regular and useful training sessions and tutorials on everything you will need but it all adds to your time. I used to do my own books as a driving instructor, filling in my own spreadsheet each week. Then at the end of each month, I would check them against the bank statements (you do have a separate business account, don't you?) Then yearly do an online submission to HMRC. Initially I let it all get behind but soon learnt my lesson and started routinely every week.

On this subject I would urge you to consider a separate bank account for your business. Preferably a business account but at least a separate one. You will find it so much easier, and easily evidencable should the need arise, to keep track of things. It might be worthwhile paying a bookkeeper an hour a week to do this for you. Put ALL your income through the account and draw out a wage. It is legally your responsibility to keep full and accurate business records, this can be by,

- An accounts ledger
- Computer spreadsheet
- Basic bookkeeping software

LEGAL
REQUIREMENTS

The following section is on some of the legal requirements you must adhere to as a self-employed Driving Instructor.

HIS MAJESTIES REVENUE AND CUSTOMS (HMRC)

The newly self-employed MUST register as self-employed within three months of commencing otherwise penalties will be charged.

- Call HMRC on **0845 915 4515**
- Or on-line at; http://www.hmrc.gov.uk/selfemployed/

TAX CREDITS

If you were or think you may need to claim tax credits you must notify the tax credits department.

Call HMRC Tax Credits office on 0845 300 3900

Or online at; http://www.hmrc.gov.uk/taxcredits/

SMOKING

It is illegal to smoke in a vehicle that is used for driving tuition[1] even if there is not a pupil in the vehicle or you are using the vehicle on a family holiday. It also affects the resale value of your vehicle as well. You may not realise how much the smell of stale smoke lingers in the vehicle. There is a move now to ban smoking at the wheel of any vehicle by any driver.

You **must** also display no smoking stickers in your vehicle by law. If an examiner feels the smell of smoke is too bad, they can refuse to take a car out on test.

I have seen many times, instructors who drive along smoking with their cigarette out the window, one guy used to come to the office and sit in his tailgate smoking outside.

I was amazed to find out, vaping is not covered under the act and as such is legally allowed to happen inside a car. I was checking because we were getting a lot of complaints from pupils and parents because one instructor kept vaping during the lessons. We asked him to stop but he refused saying it was not illegal. We tried to tell him that parents and pupils were complaining but he would not have it. He told me that I should explain to these complaining people that he is within his rights to vape in the car. (Arrogance or what). He would tell me; vaping does not give off any smoke. I still laugh today every time I see a cloud of smoke coming from some vaper's vehicle. Incidentally, the instructor does NOT work for me anymore!

MOBILE PHONES

I am sure by now we all know it is against the law to use a mobile phone or any similar communication device whilst driving or to use a mobile phone whilst supervising a learner. But it seems to escape many instructors that this includes them while sitting in a passenger seat giving instruction. This includes texting or the use of internet etc. This also includes times when you are waiting at the side of the road or stopped at traffic lights etc. Apart from the fact that it is very bad manners to use a phone while your pupil is paying for that time. Put your phone on silent or switch it off during all lessons. It could result in a fine and points on your licence, and points on your driving licence will have to be explained to the DSA who could revoke your licence to teach.

This may seem strange, but I have seen many Driving Instructors using their phone while on lessons and driving. Some I have spoken to argue that they have businesses to run and must answer their phone. I find, considering the nature of the job this attitude is so common. I do wonder what it would do to a business having a mobile phone conviction against them or worse still what it would do to the business if they were involved in a crash...

EMERGENCY CONTACT (ICE)

Have you heard of the 'ICE' scheme? The program was conceived in the mid-2000s and promoted by British paramedic Bob Brotchie in May 2005. It encourages people to enter emergency contacts in their mobile phone address book under the name "ICE" (In Case of Emergency). Not a legal requirement, but this is certainly a good idea. In case of emergency (ICE) is a program that enables first responders, such as paramedics, fire fighters, and police officers, to identify victims and contact their next of kin to obtain important medical information. Alternately, a person can list multiple emergency contacts as "ICE1", "ICE2", etc.

Source http://en.wikipedia.org/wiki/In_case_of_emergency

DATA PROTECTION

Another point that raises its head on social media often is 'do I need to be registered under the Data Protection Act?' From my research, any business (driving school) that keeps details of customers (pupils) either on paper or electronically is required to be registered with the Data Protection Act 1998.

Under the Data Protection Act 1998, individuals have a right to have a copy of the information held about them on computer and in some manual filing systems. This is known as right of subject access. If you do receive a right of subject access request, you must deal with it promptly within 40 days of receiving it. This includes all records you may have on your pupils such as progress record cards and personal data. This is a simple process and costs about £45 per year currently. This is probably one of the most common areas driving instructors bury their heads in the sand over.

DRIVING STANDARDS AGENCY (DSA) CODE OF CONDUCT

Some time ago now, the DVSA wrote a code of conduct for driving instructors. All driving instructors should read and adhere to the DSA code of conduct. This can be found by going to the following link;

http://www.dft.gov.uk/dsa/documents/dg/dsa_adi_14.pdf

Most of it is just plain good business sense and good customer relations.

NEW DRIVERS ACT

There is a legal scheme called 'The New Drivers Act'. Under the New Drivers Act your driving licence will be revoked if a driver builds up six or more penalty points within two years of passing their first driving test. They will need to reapply for their driving licence as a learner driver and re-sit their driving test.

Any penalty points they gain before passing their first driving test are considered. However, having six or more doesn't mean their licence will be revoked straight after they pass their test.

Gaining further points after passing their test, taking their total to six or more, will mean their licence will be revoked.

PUBLIC AND PROFESSIONAL LIABILITY INSURANCE

Another 'head buried in the sand' item is the need for public and professional liability insurances. Like many types of insurances, you will never appreciate their value until you need them. I am amazed how still do date; no driving instructors have been sued over their professional conduct with a pupil. We have all seen the 'had an accident, took out a mortgage' or the new one 'been delayed at an airport' no win no pay companies advertising every day. I am convinced, that one day we will have a 'have you had a crash? Were you taught properly' claim going on! If an insurance company could prove that someone was not taught using the official guides or practices, I wonder what sort of case they might bring.

PUBLIC LIABILITY

Industry and commerce are based on a range of processes and activities that have the potential to affect third parties (members of the public, visitors, trespassers, sub-contractors, etc.) who may be physically injured or whose property may be damaged or both. Regardless of this not being compulsory, instructors should include public liability insurance in their insurance portfolio even though the conditions, exclusions, and warranties included within the standard policies can be a burden.

PROFESSIONAL INDEMNITY

Professional Indemnity Insurance is compulsory for most professional businesses and services; this includes traditional professions such as architects, business consultants, engineers, insurance brokers, solicitors, independent financial advisers, accountants, computer consultants etc., as well as new insurance covers for miscellaneous classes where professional indemnity insurance protects that business's interests against claims for error, omissions and professional neglect for both the principles and their employees. It is recommended that Driving Instructors obtain this insurance as well.

FREE PUBLIC AND PROFESSIONAL LIABILITY INSURANCE

Many of the professional Driving Instructor organisations such as the ADINJC, DIA, and the MSA include these insurances as part of their membership. You will find figures of £5,000,000 and £10,000,000 being quoted as the norm but something I was told by the insurance company that runs these that, the free ones are group policies and if, for arguments sake, a member made a claim and received £4500,000 of the £5,000,000 then a future claim in that year could not exceed the total sum. It is a total for all claims in a year. Now this has not been used yet, but it could be.

Instructors with my franchise get Public and professional liability cover free. However, this cover gives each individual instructor £5,000,000 and £10,000,000 worth of cover irrespective of any other claims by any other instructor.

LESSON DELIVERY

LESSON CHARGES

I have heard many myths and poor advice amongst the forums and driving instructor communities about the way to cost a lesson. From 'ring round and charge £2.00 an hour less' to 'pitch your price in the middle'. Usually this is advice from an instructor who also complains about the cheapness of driving lessons. Let's make this clear, it is Driving Instructors who dictate the price of lessons, and it is a fundamental flaw, believing that all the pupils want is cheap lessons. (Remember don't confuse offers with cheap prices). This has been generated by a succession of Instructors who have failed to price their business properly and many of whom have now gone bust. Remember, 95% of businesses fail and 4 out of 5 instructors go bust within 2 years so if you are going to survive you MUST get this right.

You only need to look at retail trades like Lidl v Marks and Spencers food, they both sell food but why is one more expensive. Or Joes greasy spoon café v A Gordon Ramsey restaurant. Both sell food here but what more would you expect from the Gordon Ramsey restaurant. Each has their own client and the same in the driver training world. If you work for a franchise, they will be targeting a certain customer, we call them 'avatars' in business. A franchise will look to target a certain market. An independent instructor will need to do the same. It is a huge mistake to think you just want anyone and everyone. You will get nobody because nobody identifies with you. There are people that would never want to be seen in 'Joes greasy spoon' and likewise people who would never go to 'Gordon Ramsey's' restaurant, even if they could afford it.

When I was a driving instructor, I always wore a shirt and tie. Smart pressed black trousers and polished shoes. My car was immaculate and sometimes waiting for a pupil, I would give the car that extra polish. I had people from very wealthy homes seeking me out. I spoke in terms of what the Highway Code says and never ran anyone down. I had this image of authority that pupils and their parents could trust. It worked very well indeed for me. Now this might not be you but think about your ideal 'avatar' who is your ideal customer that suits you. If you want to wear flip flops and a shiny black string vest and tight shorts, don't try for the upmarket customer. You might argue that what you wear makes no difference to your teaching, and this might be true, but the fact is, you will always be judged by it. So, let's look further.

HOW TO SELL YOURSELF ON THAT FIRST LESSON

The first lesson is probably the most important lesson you will ever do for each pupil. This is the basis of my school's offer. Let's say you get them in the driving seat for just £30 (This was pre-COVID) for the two hours then give them a great lesson. They do not know you and you do not know them. Here is where your success and future lie. The pupil will be a mix of emotions; excited, nervous, dubious, cautious and many more. Ideally this will be a two-hour lesson, and, in this time, you really need to get them moving. If it's only a one-hour lesson, don't spend ages on the controls of the car as these can be covered later, just give an abridged version. Do not rush your pupil though, they will be nervous and could back off if they feel rushed. Keep calm and explain simply what you want them to do. A nice quote I heard from an instructor was how he says to his pupil, 'he will drive the car through them'. You need this pupil to go home and to school/college and say how fantastic this lesson was. If your pupil has had some lessons already, then I used to find out what they really wanted to learn from me and then I would achieve this. Often it would be manoeuvre and I would sort this out in half of the lesson and teach them something new in the other half. Either way I wanted them to know I was the right instructor for them and give them the best lesson I could. Never, I repeat, never belittle any previous training or instructor they have had before. Don't become just another instructor, **become their instructor**.

Ok, so they have had the best lesson of their lives. Now is the time to give them honest advice about their test and future lessons. You need to believe in what it is you are telling your pupils, and they will believe it too. Many times, I have had pupils and even trainees on part three who after a lesson agreed they were not ready for the previous two tests they failed with their previous instructors. This is also when you will talk to them about booking the test, how many hours you feel would be a realistic goal etc.

> *There are no secrets to this, simply let your pupils know you care about their progress and give honest advice.*

GOOD DIARY PLANNING

Many driving instructors have a very haphazard diary with lessons booked all over the place. After each driving lesson, they look at their diary to try to fit each pupil in. I remember not so long ago, doing some training with an instructor with their pupil. At the end of the lesson, the instructor and pupil were struggling to find a compatible time for the next driving lesson. In the end, they found time 3 weeks away. The pupil was very keen to have sooner. This pupil worked regular shifts, albeit rotating on a 2-week basis.

It is a good idea to try and get your pupils booked in for a regular slot each week. This avoids confusion and missed lessons. This can be changed at the pupil's request if needed. Keep one slot open per week for your driving tests. I used to keep Friday at 3.27 test slot free and 99% of pupils could do their test then. Try to fit pupil's lessons in with their college or University lessons, perhaps picking them up from home and dropping them at their college etc. Plan your diary to help minimise dead mileage, wherever possible keeping locations and appointments close. An important factor is to allow 30 minutes between lessons. This gives you time if a lesson over ran or you needed a tea break or 'pit stop.' And don't forget to allow for a proper lunch and tea breaks, it may seem obvious, but many instructors forget these things and your quality of life will soon disappear.

Don't forget to allow at least half an hour for tea breaks and

DAVE FOSTER MA, DIP.DI

lunch!

1 HOUR LESSON

On occasions you will get pupils who insist on a one-hour lesson. You should avoid this if you can, the reasons for which are outlined in the following section 'why instructors lose pupils.' Although the pupils will feel that they can only afford a one-hour lesson, you will show them they cannot afford to learn this way. If however, your pupil insists, do not refuse but you will need to be honest with them and let them know that this will take a lot longer and, in most cases, three times longer. I would suggest to my pupils who were struggling with money to take two hours every fortnight rather than one hour a week; this would at least cut down on some of the costs. I would tend to carry out these rare one-hour lessons at the beginning or end of the day to maximise diary planning.

LATE NOTICE TESTS

Often the phone will ring, and the caller will announce they have a test next week or in three days 'can you take them?' The reasons they give are varied and range from 'my normal instructor has a double booking' 'my instructor has let me down' etc. Short notice test 'can' be a bit suspicious. However, they can also be the start of something good. Many schools have a minimum amount of lessons before they will take on this short notice test sort of system. I have also seen many instructors do a simple assessment and be able to book semi-intensives in before the test or be able to postpone the test. Maybe they are ready, and the reason is genuine. Often because you have given such swift service, they will be the ones telling everyone about how good you are.

One of the 1st 4 Driving Instructors in Cornwall recently did a short notice test. The man passed, and six referrals came because of it. Now that is good business!

Do not commit to a test without having an assessment lesson first and check the driving licence thoroughly!

I was chased by a driver once in a large van who pulled up behind me in a car park and asked me to take him for his test in three days' time. I was offered a large sum of money, but I declined, and no, he was not using L plates or had a supervising driver in his sign written works van!!

FAST TRACK/ INTENSIVE

Why not? If the pupil is up to it and your diary can cope, then meet your pupil's demands. Now the reality is often they have not completed a theory test, so I would suggest they have a two-hour lesson while they apply and study for their theory test. When the theory test comes through, we look at booking the practical test on a framework that suits both you and your pupil. The reality with most test centre waiting times is that there will be an eight to ten week wait, so the two-hour weekly lessons can continue. (currently I know, test waiting times can be a lot longer, but this is written for when things get back to whatever normal is) Six weeks wait until theory plus ten weeks wait until practical gives you at least 16 two-hour lessons, which is virtually enough to pass. I spoke in an earlier chapter about meeting the pupil's needs and intensive courses can add variety and new challenges, but ensure your pupil understands that these delays may make intensive study impractical/unnecessary.

MORE ON INTENSIVE DRIVING LESSONS

Start Monday, pass Friday. What! Friday? You may have seen adverts like this advertising driving lessons. Oh, how driving instructors often like to complain about them. How can they guarantee this? Nobody can pass that quickly, and many more type complaints. They forget it's just marketing.

For over 10 years, part of my business is looking after not only my own driving schools, but other driving schools. From simply the call answering to the actual website, promotion, and marketing. Along the way we have helped and worked with several specialist intensive driving schools and one or two that do both weekly and intensive driving lessons. This gives me some insight as to the operation and pros and cons of the intensive market.

INTENSIVES ARE NOT FAIRIES!

One of the most common things I hear when talking to driving instructors is 'I don't believe in them'. This often makes me chuckle as they really do exist LOL. It's not like fairies you know. (Sorry for all the fairy believers I've just upset). I think what people mean is, they don't believe they work, or they are not good for the pupil. The simple fact is, they do work some of the time for some of the people. But they don't always work, and they don't work for all the people. Now I know the last two sentences say the same thing in effect, but I think it's important to realise they can work but not always. Got it? Right! I will move on.

There are driving schools and instructors up and down the country who are successfully delivering intensive driving lessons and have been for a long time. For some learners it's the best way they learn. For some learners it's the best way they can learn to drive because of work commitments. For some learners they just simply would not do it if they could not do it in a large block. I know many prolific blog writers who write all their blogs together, then schedule them to be posted weekly, it's the way some people work. I'm not aware of any evidence, apart from the training of military personnel, that intensives are any less safe or make worse drivers. There is research to do with military personnel, but I think this is because they use the one size fits all and train everyone intensively. The argument for works equally against for the military type training. Some people simply do not benefit from this type of intensive

DAVE FOSTER MA, DIP.DI

training.

ARE THEY A PROBLEM?

Well sometimes they are. And when they are a problem, the problems are often worse than with normal weekly driving lessons. Let's take for example a pupil who is not feeling well. They wake in the morning, as we all have, streaming with a cold. Now if this was a weekly one- or two-hour driving lessons, that's what they may or may not cancel. The die fast will be 'you have to pay even if you die'. Many of us consider whether to charge and often give the benefit of the doubt for good rapport and customer relationship. But in an intensive, this could be a whole day or more worth of income. This gets harder. The same feelings occur and thought processes must be dealt with by the driving instructor but now it's a whole lot more money. Possibly make or break. Few can absorb such a high loss of income so charges must be made, and here is the biggest problem because now you do need to get ready for a complaint. Likewise, the pupil can't afford such a loss in income and likewise will not give up so easily. Often parents get involved pleading for their children and complaining it's not their fault. And a massive dilemma occurs. Couple all this to the fact that, they might have their driving test coming up shortly and there may not be enough diary time to make up the lost hours. They might have taken time of work, and this all compounds the problem and gets stressful. Talking of stressful, we all know that stress can bring on illness. Pressure can bring on stress and a pupil that has a deadline, feels they are not going to make that deadline starts to get stressed and then starts to feel ill. They then need to cancel, and this circle starts again. This is just one of the reasons why pupils may need to cancel. Other outside factors such as death or illness in the family, work commitment or child commitments changing are a few more. The fact is, if there is a problem, they can be worse with intensive driving courses.

THEN THERE'S THE INSTRUCTOR

We've all had that rare problem where we've had a car breakdown or are own illness or family problem. With weekly driving lessons, we call the pupil and cancel or re-schedule the driving lesson for the following week. Like the pupil though, if we need to cancel an intensive driving lesson, we are talking of maybe a day or more. Get ready for the phone to ring with a complaint. Here in the office, we have dealt with many of these. An instructor whose father died, and instructor who had a heart attack and another who had a serious car crash, the phone rang for all these with complaints. All pupils/parents expecting the driving lessons and tests to still go ahead. Now it might be possible to sort another car out but even the best companies take a day or two, but do we have driving instructors on standby, err no! Again, to be fair the pupils end up stressed and worrying about their time constraints etc.

Suffice to say, whatever the problems you get with weekly driving lessons, they are compounded and worse for intensives. The slow learner will appear slower, the unreliable pupil appears more unreliable. They take a lot of managing and we have found you need the right driving instructors. Something as a driving school I would insist is that instructors are not paid until the course or at least parts of it have been completed. This would certainly have saved so many problems with the intensive driving schools we have worked with. Schools have paid instructors before the course, for one reason the driving instructor has not completed or even started the driving course and has refused to give the school owner back the money. Possibly because in their opinion the pupil let them down, but many have resulted in huge complaints. The school can't give the money back because they don't have it, the instructor can't or won't and the pupil uses something called a charge back on their credit or debit card they paid with. The bank without question re-claws the money back from the driving school who have ten days to prove the pupil had the driving lessons or defaulted in some way and often this is difficult to prove. More so if there is no contract between school and pupil and even worse if no contract between school and instructor. This is all followed of course by a damming review on social media.

WHEN THINGS GO WELL

Like mentioned earlier, some pupils excel with this type of learning. The process for many is good. Rather than spreading the process over many weeks where during those weeks the likelihood of an illness is greater or any other problems increased, simply because they are taken over a shorter timescale. Often pupils will, muddle on through with a minor cold or complaint where is it was just a two-hour lesson, would have cancelled. There is as much riding on this for the pupils as the driving instructors. We have seen many pupils excel with this type of training. Passing tests in a short number of driving lessons simply because the style suited their individual learning style. They learn in record number of hours and feel the experience was fantastic. Great reviews follow and others see how 'Fred passed an intensive with only 15 driving lessons.' (Is that lessons or hours). The phone starts ringing because this looks good.

AH, THE PUPILS' EXPECTATIONS.

I'm sure many of the problems come from the pupils' expectations. We have all seen the adverts, 'Start Monday pass Friday.' This is a marketing ploy often and with my marketing hat on, a good one. There is a demand for this, a problem, so why not fill the demand and create a solution for the problem. However, with my driving instructor hat on, this is not a good marketing ploy. Pupils believe they will all start this Monday and pass five days later the following Friday. The adverts don't say what Friday or for that matter what Monday they will start. Pupils see their friends have done it so it must work for them too. Remember though, it does not work for all the pupils all the time. A pupil books a 30-hour course, because 'that's all they can afford' gets halfway through and it's apparent they will need more driving lessons. Dilemma ahead as they can't afford more. Up go the stress levels, on comes the illness and here we go again. Trying to realistically give an answer to the question 'how many driving lessons will I need?' is impossible, well giving a truthful one anyway.

How many driving lessons will I need = 3 x 3.14/9.7 x age x the length of a piece of string.

THE JOYS OF MARKETING INTENSIVE DRIVING LESSONS

Certainly, there is a demand for intensive driving lessons. All my career as an instructor I advertised these as I found they were a much-searched term on the search engines. They brought in many pupils asking about intensive driving lessons, and I signed most of them up. How many intensive driving courses have I delivered? NONE, not one. They have always gone the same way for me. I ask them if they have their theory booked. Normally this is a no, so I suggest we do a few lessons leading up to the theory to 'get their hand in and make the intensive easier.' They normally go for this and when the theory is passed, just carry on with the weekly driving lessons. Simples!

Then there is another aspect to cover. Like anything, if there is a niche market, people do expect to pay more. Some driving schools seem to get confused on this with block bookings. I know it's common practice to discount blocks of driving lessons, it's one I do myself as there are good marketing reasons for this but don't discount intensive driving lessons. I have had schools charging and filling diaries at £50 an hour for intensive driving lessons. Of course, it's hidden in the total price with the included driving tests etc. I'm sure pupils just don't do the maths and work out what they are paying for, but they are getting a niche market. They get their driving instructors sole attention for the week or so of the course. It's a market winner and will remain so for many years. They can fit in very well with an instructor's lifestyle too as often they are Monday to Friday 10am-4pm.

Intensive driving lessons are and always will be controversial. Like Marmite, you either love it or hate it. What is important though is the way they are managed. They need to be managed firmly and tactfully. Never promise what you can't fulfil and remember the reality of expectations. Contracts are a must for both instructors and pupils just in case of problems. I have seen this go right many times and go wrong. When it goes wrong in can go wrong big style and the stress it causes... have I mentioned stress?

Let me tell you a sad story. A few years ago now, a school we were working with did lots of intensive courses. A pupil whose lessons were, well being paid for my Her Majesties Government turned up on a Monday morning for his intensive driving lessons. Now for some reason, the school owner had forgotten or had just not booked the test. The instructor simply refused to take the guy out. The instructor had been paid already and the school owner refused to pay the money back. As we were dealing with all the phone calls for this school, it was us who were called and asked why. The school owner refused to speak to them. I started getting some more official calls from the home office and then the police. The only way I had to get hold of the school owner was email or text. The police found 5 telephone numbers for the school owner and every single one diverted back to my number. Well, you can imagine my messages and emails at the time. The police I know, searched photos of test passes from the school owner trying to get a registration and an address. The one listed was old and not current. Not one photo showed his car registration. I believe they got him in the end as I simply got a call from the police saying they won't need to contact me anymore; they have resolved it. Hey, the school is still trading today!

Types of payment

I have said before that driving instructors need to think of themselves as business first and trainers second. Never has this been truer than taking payments. Let's look at this. You are in business for money, yes, we love our job and relish the way our learners grow and achieve new skills, but we need money to run our businesses and pay our bills. It is with this in mind, I never cease to be amazed how many obstacles driving instructors put in the way of allowing their customers to pay. Initially, this was a cash business but driving schools saw an opportunity to use credit cards etc. to take block bookings. Many driving instructors have now gone on to say their pupils can only pay by online banking now. I've mentioned this to two business groups I belong to and they are amazed as to why anyone in business would want to put obstacles in the way of anyone paying. As an instructor you need to be able to take payment in almost any form. If you are with a franchise, there is a good chance they will take payments by debit/credit card etc. for you and pay it directly to you. Usually, they absorb any card fees in the franchise payments. I sit here and think about how I pay for things. I almost always use my credit card that we pay off at the end of each month. One, we get bonuses for using it and two, we get extra protection if things go wrong. I would certainly advise pupils to pay by credit card as I have seen only too close up, where things have gone wrong, and the instructor has taken the money. Those that paid by credit card, did a simple claw back and received all their money back. Now when I say advise, I don't say this to every pupil just here for the readers of this book. Each month as a driving school, we take many thousands of pounds in payments on behalf of our instructors, proof that there is a need for card payments and if you don't offer this, you will miss out.

Cash is still a favourite with some pupils although I advise not keeping large quantities in the car, unfortunately, it's such an obvious place for thieves to target. It is rare today to see a cheque however, these are made payable to you. Bank and building society members of the UK Domestic Cheque Guarantee Card Scheme have removed the Scheme on 30th June 2011, meaning that it is no longer possible to guarantee a cheque under the Scheme.

Online payments are an option but only if this is what your pupil prefers, we offer it as a driving school but very few chose it to pay. Although this was pre-COVID. Currently most are now happy to pay by card in advance although I suspect this might change later, when the post-COVID pupil rush dies settles down. PayPal is another option, as are many of the new app type payments schemes being introduced. A word on postal orders, if you get one, frame it as I've not seen one since I was 12.

NOTE ON PAYMENTS.

I was at a meeting once for business entrepreneurs, the subject of driving schools not taking credit and debit cards came up. Not from me but from a very successful businessman and author who found his children's driving instructor did not take cards. Why would a business put hurdles in the way of customers paying money, was his statement? The group found it strange that any business wouldn't want to take cards in this day and age.

TAKE PAYMENT UP FRONT?

It is a good idea to take payment at the beginning rather than the end of the lesson. In any event, at least take the money for the lesson on the day of the test up front as there is nothing worse than taking a pupil home from a failed test and then saying, *'and that will be £40 please'*. Certainly, establish how the lesson is to be paid. Occasionally you will get to the end of a lesson and 17-year-olds being 17 will suddenly remember they wanted to go to the cash point. At least if this is decided at the beginning it can be used as a real-life training situation during the lesson. Don't allow payment to be deferred – under 18's cannot be chased for debt and even if your students are older, it is an unnecessary hassle you could do without.

Another recent idea from the forums is that all pupils pay for lessons in advance before the instructor even goes to pick them up for the lesson. The notion being that this will cut down on cancellations. Pre COVID, we found this often a hindrance in booking the lessons, it will cut down on cancellations, BUT it also cuts down on the number of pupils coming through. In the office we often go through the booking process then go to take the money on booking only to be told 'I don't have my card with me'. We find a lot of resistance to this. I calculate that you might cut down on one cancellation every couple of months, but you lose at least one pupil a week. Having said that, post COVID we are now finding pupils readily prepared and ok to pay up front. Whether this will return to the pre-COVID reluctance or not remains to be seen. There are certainly a lot of easier ways of preventing the odd cancellation.

I wonder how many people would be happy to pay for their car service, hairdressers, meal out or food shopping etc. up front.

An important lesson for me was learnt over bulk lessons in my first year of trading. It was just before Christmas, and I was selling a lot of 12-hour blocks of lessons. Instead of letting the pupil pay the driving school, I took the payments and put them in my own bank. Christmas came and I had a great Christmas with lots of presents for my children and food and drink. Then after Christmas I had to deliver all the lessons paid for by the pupils. It was one of the worst few months as a driving instructor. I had spent all the money and was writing cheques for fuel and was going into unauthorized overdrafts. Cash pupils paid for the fuel then so I could just deliver the advanced paid pupils. From that day forward I would always let my franchise take payment and pay me after the lessons were complete. When I was independent, I paid the money into a separate account and drew the money out only after I had completed the lessons. Being self-employed takes a lot of discipline sometimes and a good franchise can often help with this.

CHAPTER 6: GOOD PEDAGOGIES (LESSON PLANNING)

First few lessons

Don't be worried if you feel nervous delivering your first few lessons. Everyone is, and your pupils will not notice. Planning is the key. If you have not already done so in your training, it is a good idea to find out what routes you will be using for your learners. Just like a music teacher who starts everyone off on the same piece of music and then progresses through each piece as the learning develops. You too will find it easier to have set routes where each item on your learner's syllabus can be practiced in relative safety. From there, you can gradually amend each route as you learn from and reflect on your teachings. Below I will give you some brief outlines of the features you are looking for in each different route. It may be that if you cover a large area or different towns you will need to do this for each place but try to keep the number of areas down if you can even if you need to drive your pupils to a suitable location for the first few lessons.

NURSERY ROUTES

If you want to remain confident and focused, you need to select initial routes that have very little traffic on them. Look for wide roads with not too many junctions on them. Ideally, a few small gradients to help develop clutch control. A few simple left and right turns should be present to help develop the car controls too. Look for longer straight roads to develop the use of the gears, both up and down. Avoid traffic lights, roundabouts and pedestrian crossings or difficult road junctions that might alarm your pupil in these early lessons.

INTERMEDIATE ROUTES

Intermediate routes should lead on from or ideally overlap your nursery routes. Here we are looking for some 'give way' and 'stop' junctions, as well as basic crossroads. Some junctions on slight gradients are a good idea too, as they're slightly higher for hill/controlled start situations. Begin looking for the traffic light-controlled junctions and simple roundabouts. Here you can begin to look for the areas where you'll start to teach the manoeuvres, bearing in mind these will need to be relatively traffic-free areas initially. Try to avoid multi-lane roads, one-way streets and roundabouts that do not comply with basic rules as well as very busy right turns.

ADVANCED ROUTES

Here you are looking to extend your intermediate routes to incorporate everything else. Multi-lane roads, one-way streets and complex junctions all need to be found. It is here you will look to develop your mock test routes too.

GENERAL ROUTE ADVICE

Try to avoid test routes as much as possible and look for areas where there are not too many learners practicing. In recent years there has been a lot of bad publicity about Driving Instructors using the same areas and residents are often complaining to the test centre managers and press. If you do see learners practicing, try to move on to another area as best you can. Never get confrontational with a resident, if they ask you to move on or are seen watching you just smile and take an alternate route. In time, you will build up your training areas and will seek out new, challenging areas. New areas where there are not too many learners are good for business too as yours will be the only car seen. When possible, try to build a good rapport with areas and residents by using common courtesy. You never know where your next pupil will be coming from...

THE WRONG ROAD!

I remember on one of my early lessons, missing a right turn and ending up on a no through road, feeling very embarrassed I quickly suggested a 'turn in the road' it really was a narrow road, and it must have taken at least 8 turns to get the car round. In Exeter there used to be a problem with a roundabout under the M5 motorway where pupils on their test would be told by the examiner 'follow the road ahead, take the third exit, sign posted Exmouth' Pupils would get confused and take the second exit and unless the examiner was quick, they would end up going up the slip road to the M5 motorway! Many a test was then abandoned as the examiner had no choice but to walk back to the test centre with the pupil.

LESSON STRUCTURE

Some of the subjects covered in this section might seem odd as 'lesson structure', but we need to take the structure and look at it holistically or all the different parts. Remember, we are businesspeople first and driving instructors second.

One of the main reasons pupils leave instructors is, they just don't feel like they are making progress. Instructors often have a hap hazard or weak approach to their lesson structure. It contains many elements, some of which are not obvious. I know some pupils take longer and some a lot longer, but we need to make sure they know they are making progress. Let's look at some research I did a long time ago. There are many reasons given to instructors as why they want to leave, I'm having a break, I can't afford it, my mum says etc. But my research showed the following were given by pupils in an anonymous research call.

- *'My instructor kept shouting at me'*
- *'My instructor was smelly'*
- *'They always turned up late'*
- *'They kept getting angry'*
- *'The car was always dirty'*
- *'My instructor was scruffy'*
- *'They just turned up and we drove round a bit'*

These are just a few examples of the reasons given by the pupils. Not once did pupils say anything about giving up because they couldn't afford them. This is backed up by something I heard from the DVSA at the time, that pupils take 47 hours of driving lessons on average with 22 hours of private practice using on average 3 instructors.

However, by far the two most common reasons for leaving their 'previous instructor' are *'I did not feel I was making progress'* **or** *'I did not have any goals.'* These two are so easily dealt with by good lesson planning. Always set objectives for your lessons and another tip I will cover soon, book the test in advance.

PROGRESS SHEETS OR RECORD CARDS

It is amazing how many instructors do not use record cards or progress reports of any form. I hear things such as 'I can remember' or 'I don't like filling in paperwork' but these are for the pupil as much as for the instructor. Always filling in the progress sheet at the end of every lesson shows the learner what has been achieved and what still needs to be achieved. It is a great way, however small progress, you can show the pupil, who in turn could show their parents any progress.

Fill in the record card with the pupil, don't just fill it in but involve the pupil. Ask them how they felt they did in aspects. Often, they feel they have not done so well so now is a chance to show them what they have done. Don't be over realistic either. You need time to show they have improved. Someone might have done very well today but don't give them the very top marks, they get those for consistently achieving in that area. Here is an area, I think driving instructors go a little wrong sometimes. They cover a subject with a pupil, mark it off as 'done' and that's that. No subject is 'done' until they can consistently demonstrate it over many lessons in different circumstances. Here is another chance to allow the pupils to take responsibility for their own learning.

COST, HOW TO SELL THE BEST TYPE OF DRIVING LESSON

As mentioned earlier, you need to let your pupils know you have their best interest at heart, and they will trust you. It's about getting that all important rapport needed to be able to teach them. I have talked previously of the two-hour lesson and its benefits; well, this is how you sell it to your pupils and show them the best way forward.

A one-hour lesson has just one half an hour learning period in it. You have 15 minutes at the beginning of 'How are you, how is mum?' etc. followed by a half an hour learning period. Then 15 minutes at the end spent debriefing, taking the payment, and booking the next lesson.

ONE-HOUR LESSON

15 Mins Intro	30 Mins Learning period	15 Mins Debrief

A two-hour lesson has the same 15 minutes at the beginning and at the end but three 30-minute learning periods. This has effectively three times the learning for only twice the cost.

TWO-HOUR LESSON

15 Mins Intro	30 Mins Learning period	30 Mins Learning period	30 Mins Learning period	15 Mins Debrief

You are showing your learners how they can save money and learn quicker.

HOW MUCH DOES YOUR PUPIL WANT TO PAY?

I always used to ask my pupils '*how much do you want to pay*?' The answer will always be along the lines of '*as little as possible*'. I would ask them if they had read about how many driving lessons the DVSA say is the average. It is common that they have read 45-47hrs etc. I would use an example of the DVSA average at 47 lessons. Showing that 47 lessons at an average £30 would cost them £1,645, I would point out that this was an average and they may need only half of them, particularly as they are young and probably still studying. They would still see that this would be £822.50. I would then use the example about two-hour lessons, showing that this would effectively reduce the required lessons by a third (33%). This would mean if around 15 two-hour lessons were needed, you would expect it to cost on average £1,050. I would always keep saying, this is the DVSA research and I have always found that pupils doing two-hour lessons will take a lot less. I would then suggest they used block booking so that further savings could be made…they of course are thinking that they will only need half that (as I had suggested earlier) so the reality of them affording them is getting easier. What I am doing is having a conversation WITH them, showing how I will help them.

I would always write this down on some paper while I did this for the pupil to keep and so the pupil can see the logic for themselves and to give to their parents later. Tailor this to the pupil, a pupil who's had 30 lessons already will need a different quote. The example I used reflects a new pupil with no prior experience.

NO GOAL (BOOK THE PUPILS TEST)

My example above would follow on by asking them *'when would you like to pass your test.'* Answers of *'as soon as possible'* can be expected. Again, use the example of the DSA average of 47 hours of tuition. If a pupil was to take one x 1 hour driving lesson a week, this would mean the average pupil would take one year (50 weeks with holidays). Do you think you could keep all your pupils that long? I couldn't. Use the two-hour lesson and you are only looking at about four months until the test. As your pupil will be trying to halve this (most seem to feel that they are better than the average) then they are thinking about two months, a time frame almost any pupil will be happy with. As before I will write this down on the same piece of paper, giving them an actual date in my diary for when I would expect them to sit their practical test in about 16 weeks. (Current post COVID times not possible, but it will return to normal eventually)

Let's take a step back. In schools and colleges, when you sign up for a course the exam dates are set in stone. You work towards these dates and take extra tuition or do extra study to meet these dates. So why does this not happen with driving tuition? In my experience, you can book up your pupil's test dates well in advance and work towards that goal. This follows with the theory test too, I book this for the pupil if they have not already done it, generally aiming for about 6 weeks time. You need to be a little guided by the pupil as some have learning difficulties and this time frame may not suit them, but overall, 6 weeks is fine for most.

So, who books the tests? Simple! You do. So many instructors leave the pupil to book their own test and then experience problems such as double bookings, pupils booking too soon or booking when you are away etc.

PROFESSIONAL
OR COWBOY

Imagine having a builder come to your house and say, *'you get the materials and let me know when you have them, then I will come and build your extension any time to suit you...'* What are we thinking, professional or cowboy?

What about a plumber who comes and gives you a quote for a new radiator and says *'you go to B&Q (other good retailers of bathroom fittings do exist) and get the radiator and I will fit it when you want...'* Again, what's your opinion going to be, professional or cowboy?

Yet so many instructors say, *'you go and book your test and let me know when it is, and I will do it...'* and then complain that their pupil has been apparently 'ripped off' by some test booking agency that charges them extra to book the test for them! I am not saying these agencies are good, but they are providing a service that most Driving Instructors won't. It is very clear by the amount of pupils that use these services that there is a market for them. Who should be providing those services? Is there a marketing advantage here?

Booking a test is simple using your unique business ID and the dedicated number, which speed dials directly to a DVSA operator. Book the theory test for them, the day after their first lesson for about six weeks time and when they pass, book the practical test for about 10 weeks after that, which will be roughly 16 weeks from their first lesson with you.

So, what have we now got? A pupil who has had their first lesson and is excited at driving the car for the first time, they go home to Mum and Dad and tell them all about it and how the instructor has booked both their theory and practical test (in YOUR diary). Mum and Dad are happy as they would have been worried about how long it would take and how much it would cost. When they go to school, they tell their friends who are amazed that their test is being booked and wonder why their instructor has not booked their test.

Your pupil not only has a goal but a way to achieve this goal and all they must do is turn up for their regular lessons. Your pupils won't leave you because you are providing what they want. It is the instructors who give no real timescale and just wander through lessons who lose their pupils.

I believe the above is so important, as an instructor for 1st 4 Driving, we in the office will book the driving tests for our instructors' pupils. We can book it straight into their diary and avoid any double bookings.

The 17 standards required to deliver a good lesson.

For some time now, we have had the standards from the DVSA for teaching pupils to drive and how driving instructors are marked. The fit into 3 categories,

- LESSON PLANNING
- RISK MANAGEMENT
- TEACHING AND LEARNING STRATEGIES

Instructors are graded on each standard 0-3

- 0 = No evidence shown
- 1 = Demonstrated in a few elements
- 2 = Demonstrated in most elements
- 3 = Demonstrated in all elements

A score of less than 30 results in a fail, 31-42 gets a grade B and 43-51 a grade A. Note, 7 or less in the risk management is an automatic fail. I could dedicate a whole book to the standards alone but here I will cover them briefly. So let's look at what each individual standard is.

LESSON PLANNING

DID THE TRAINER IDENTIFY THE PUPIL'S LEARNING GOALS AND NEEDS?

You need to identify the goals of the lesson, not only at the beginning but if you need to change the plan. Too many instructors set no real goals at the beginning and even less as they go through the lesson. Let's say you start off setting a goal for today's lesson as 'routine on approach to roundabouts.' During this lesson, your pupil starts having slight problems with the clutch. You might set a mini goal of 'for the next 5 minutes we will work on your clutch control'. This gives the pupil something to achieve in 5 minutes. Throughout the lesson, you will often change or set goals.

A goal is just something you and the pupil agree to cover. If you are setting goals and achieving them, progress must be being made.

WAS THE AGREED LESSON STRUCTURE APPROPRIATE FOR THE PUPIL'S EXPERIENCE AND ABILITY?

Choosing a level that meets the learner's ability can seem confusing. Let's look at our example used above with the routine on approach to roundabouts. Teaching roundabouts to a pupil who can't use the clutch properly is no good. So, you could be using too high a level. A very common thing to see on Standards tests, is the instructor teaching subjects when the basics are still not there. Likewise, you could be teaching at a basic level, too much telling, for a more experienced driver. Someone who is almost at test level, might need a greater amount of Q&A. When planning the lesson, consider what level will you need to use?

WERE THE PRACTICE AREAS SUITABLE?

Route planning is vitally important. You need to have enough in the route to teach what you are teaching. But consider what else is on the route. You might think of a brilliant area to teach those junctions but consider what the pupil might have to do to get there. Likewise, you need to ensure that for more advanced pupils, the route is challenging enough. I have seen occasions where the instructor has gone round the same block 10 times and not achieving anything. Consider, if the lesson goes well, how can I change the route to meet different goals.

The Practice area on a standard or part three test is different in that it will start from the test centre. You will need to think carefully about the area and equally as important, how you will get there.

WAS THE LESSON PLAN ADAPTED WHEN APPROPRIATE, TO HELP THE PUPIL WORK TOWARDS THEIR LEARNING GOALS?

Another common area for test failure is not adapting the goals. Go back to my example. Here, although the goal was initially set as 'routine on approach to roundabouts' it was clear the pupil needed some help on the clutch, so change the plan. You don't necessarily need to change the whole plan. You could just for example say, change the goal to working on the clutch for 5 or 10 minutes. Returning after to the roundabouts once the clutch is sorted. You might need to change the goal a few times and if this is what is needed by the pupil, then that's okay. Instructors often think, I have said I will do xyz, and feel they will be marked down if they don't achieve xyz. If you see something that needs sorting, sort it there and then. I hear instructors say they'll cover that next lesson but think about it, at the end of THIS lesson, the pupil will still have that problem with the clutch. How can they truly achieve the roundabouts if the clutch work is poor? Don't play lip service to it either and think, we've covered that before. Maybe you have but it's here again and you'll need to sort it.

RISK MANAGEMENT

DID THE TRAINER ENSURE THAT THE PUPIL FULLY UNDERSTOOD HOW THE RESPONSIBILITY FOR RISK WOULD BE SHARED?

It is important to let your pupil know the risk will be shared. That the responsibility to a given subject will be shared and by how much. A great way of doing this is by scaling. Giving a number from 1-5 or 1-10 or anything else as a scale, so the pupil knows where they are and where you are. Now, we can now start to transfer the responsibility bit by bit to the pupil. It's called the transfer of learning. A beginner pupil will need to know you are taking responsibility for the risk mainly, a pupil near test standard should be taking all the responsibility for the risk. As pupils cover more subjects from their syllabus, they will be taking on more and more responsibility. A pupil might have 10 out of 10 responsibilities for moving off, but 1 out of 10 for roundabouts and so on until every subject is covered and they can demonstrate, over a period of time, they can keep doing the subject continuously without error.

Break responsibilities down further if needed. A pupil could be responsible for left junctions but not right, for the mirrors and signal on approach but not the position, speed or look. There are infinite variables to this. What's important, is you start giving responsibility as and when you can.

WERE THE DIRECTIONS AND INSTRUCTIONS GIVEN TO THE PUPIL CLEAR AND GIVEN IN GOOD TIME?

Sitting in the back of many driving lessons, it never ceases to amaze me, the many different way instructors give route direction. I remember a forum post asking why examiners do not give route directions like instructors. Well, there must be a standard way, otherwise the pupils will get confused. Examiners all use roughly the same terminology. Having all been trained, and regularly checked to the same standard. As there are many different varieties of instructor versions, it stands to reason we should use the same as the examiners. Instructors are not doing pupils any favours in using directions like 'hang a left here' or 'go over the roundabout and turn right' etc. Sit in the back of driving tests and listen to the examiner. They use a system like ADI

Alert, I would like you to

Direct, turn right

Identify, at the next junction

Alert, At the roundabout

Direct, I would like you to follow the road ahead

Identify, the second exit

Sometimes, a qualifier might be given such as 'after the post box' or 'by the big fence, where maybe there might be a confusion. Do watch out for the 'I would like you to turn left at the next 'available' junction.' The word available, hints of a hidden turning or a no-entry road first.

WAS THE TRAINER AWARE OF THE SURROUNDINGS AND THE PUPIL'S ACTIONS?

We need to concentrate and be aware of everything the pupil is doing and what's going on around. Yes, you need to look out the big window at the front but are you aware what's following or what's coming out the side roads. Looking at the pupil and following them through each routine to ensure you don't miss anything. Spending a lot of time working with trainee driving instructors and looking at their failure sheets, a common area was that they just missed many of the faults. The pupil or I as a role-playing pupil, could make faults while the trainee instructor looked out the front, blissfully unaware of what was happening. The pupil can get away with murder if you're not watching for it. As I said, there is not enough time in this book to cover everything in detail, but this was the secret to mine, and those that I've trained success, was in teaching instructors to spot every fault, every time. And being aware of the surroundings.

WAS ANY VERBAL OR PHYSICAL INTERVENTION BY THE TRAINER TIMELY AND APPROPRIATE?

It's interesting that this standard follows the previous one. If you are not aware of what your pupil is doing, then you might not be until it's too late, when you do spot it and you're having to act. An action that could have been avoided if you had been aware earlier. I've seen it plenty of times, the trainee stops the pupil before turning into a no-entry road at the last minute. When mentioned they say 'but I did see it, that's why I stopped them'. Had they been more alert earlier, they might've been proactive and just used a bit of Q&A. One of our greatest 'dual controls' is our voice. Instructors often react late and dual a pupil where an earlier voice may have been more appropriate.

WAS SUFFICIENT FEEDBACK GIVEN TO HELP THE PUPIL UNDERSTAND ANY POTENTIAL SAFETY CRITICAL INCIDENTS?

Feedback is any information you give to your pupils about anything at any time during the lesson. Often instructors think this applies solely to a 'debrief' at the end. If your pupil makes a fault, you need to feed this back to them straight away if practical, or as soon afterwards as practical. Feedback needs to be sufficient. Not just a brief 'I've told you about that before' or 'we covered that before.' I hear this and similar so often during training. The instructor thinks they have covered the fault before and so a simple reminder is enough. This is so wrong because clearly the problem or fault is still there and will need 'sufficient feedback'. This could range from Q&A to ascertain understanding and cause or maybe there is a need to change the lesson plan to deal with it fully. I go back to our roundabout example, asking how we should bring the clutch up when moving off, might get an answer of, 'I'm struggling a bit' from the pupil. Here is a perfect opportunity to change the plan for 5-10 minutes to sort the clutch. By not doing this, you have not fed back enough information (feedback), sufficient to analyse the problem.

TEACHING
& LEARNING
STRATEGIES

WAS THE TEACHING STYLE SUITED TO THE PUPIL'S LEARNING STYLE AND CURRENT ABILITY?

As driving instructors, I like to think that the styles or methods we use are like different tools in our toolbox.

- Full talk through
- Demonstration
- Guided practice
- Prompted practice
- Question and answers
- Allowing pupil to just try
- Independent practice

These are some of the main tools in our toolbox. Picking the right tool for the job is the skill we acquire when training. If one tool seems unsuccessful, then try another. Avoid banging away with the same tool. 'I've told my pupil a thousand times to check their mirrors, why do they keep forgetting' is a common type of question often asked in forums. The clue of course is in the 'I TOLD them a thousand times.'

There are some guidelines that can be used. A new subject is 'likely' to need more guidance, and something that has prior knowledge and skill, is 'likely' to need Q&A. However, a lot of this depends on your learners own 'personal' learning preferences. Some learners are more kinaesthetic, this means they learn best from doing. Whereas other learners might be more auditory in that they learn from listening or visual who like demonstrations or diagrams. You can ask pupils how they prefer to learn and get an idea of how to start. Pupils will often respond to a mix of different levels though and as you gain experience; you will find out what works.

Suffice to say, if you have a pupil struggling with something and you keep on with one method, you are likely to lose marks here and your pupil will get frustrated and not learn.

WAS THE PUPIL ENCOURAGED TO ANALYSE PROBLEMS AND TAKE RESPONSIBILITY FOR THEIR LEARNING?

If you want responsible drivers, we need to give them responsibility. Today's teaching should not just be about 'telling them a thousand times', but asking questions to bring out a greater understanding of why we do something. At this point I stress, the why is not about passing a test. The why is something that will allow them to see the danger, risk, or reason why this is done beyond a driving test.

- Why do we check our mirrors?
- Why do we need to know what's behind us?
- Why is a vehicle too close to us going to be a problem?
- What does the Highway Code tell us about vehicles too close?
- What can you do about this?
- When are drivers most likely to drive too close to us?
- When are you most likely to stop using your mirrors regularly?

- What could you do to prevent this?

The above list of questions is not a definitive list, you might not ask those specific questions or all at once, but it shows you how we can create a deeper understanding of that simple 'checking the mirrors.' Whatever the subject, fault, or risk, you can use questions to get your pupil to have a better understanding of why they do something rather than just because you say so. You will only get answers from your pupils though, if you have developed a good rapport with them. One examiner I know, often talks about 'drilling the reasons why down' so you're really getting to the bottom of the problem and risk. Not just a cursory, 'why is that dangerous?' I think this is great advice.

WERE OPPORTUNITIES AND EXAMPLES USED TO CLARIFY LEARNING OUTCOMES?

Looking back at our example lesson on roundabouts where the pupil developed a clutch problem. If you change the plan and work on the clutch, you are giving the pupil opportunities to work on the problem. Look at another. Your pupil is doing meeting traffic, and they drive too close to a parked car. Here you might ask them about how close they should pass parked cars. You might decide to change the plan and go around the block to find an example of where to practice or teach adequate clearance. After a few minutes you might return to the original parked car giving opportunity for the pupil to pass the car correctly. Using real life on-road scenarios is a good way of improving skill and knowledge. Something a classroom teacher often never gets a chance to do with their pupils.

WAS THE TECHNICAL INFORMATION GIVEN COMPREHENSIVE, APPROPRIATE, AND ACCURATE?

Ask 10 driving instructors a question and you'll often get 10 different answers. It's amazing how many instructors will give different answers to what seem like basic questions. When I was training instructors, I did a lot of work with trainees who had previously failed with other driving schools, so often I was told strange things. How often must you check your mirrors, was a regular 'test' question I used. The answer would vary from 'every 2 to 10 seconds.' I would follow up with 'what does the Highway Code say', and rarely could anyone tell me the correct answer. And this is just one example. Often trainees would get frustrated and say, 'I don't know what to say as you are telling me something different to my trainer.' 'I'm not telling you anything' I would say, I'm asking you what the Highway Code says, you can give the examiner on your part three anything you want, 2 seconds, 8 seconds or what the Highway Code says, what would your pupil and examiner prefer to hear?

Accurate knowledge is essential and should always be from the approved books. If every instructor used them, there wouldn't be so many differences in opinion. Study your subject well and keep the textbooks with you. You can't be expected to remember everything, so if a pupil asks you something technical ask 'where can we find this information?' Now you're also starting to teach your pupil where they can find the information for themselves after their driving lessons once they have passed.

WAS THE PUPIL GIVEN APPROPRIATE AND TIMELY FEEDBACK DURING THE SESSION?

In the risk management section, we looked at 'Was sufficient feedback given to help the pupil understand any potential safety critical incidents?' Now we look at 'was that feedback given at the right time and was it the correct feedback for the situation?'. Another common fault I see is a pupil is approaching a junction or something else that requires the pupil's concentration, and the instructor starts talking about something else. Give the route direction and allow the pupil to do the task. However, if there is a potential risk, then you might need to say something. This is about saying the right thing at the right time. You aren't concentrating, and your pupil starts to turn into a no entry road, you use the dual controls. Your feedback was not well timed, and it was not appropriate. To have used a little Q&A earlier would have been better timed and more appropriate. Another tip is when pupils do something not so well, to just telling them what to do would be not appropriate when Q&A would have been better.

WERE THE PUPILS' QUERIES FOLLOWED UP AND ANSWERED?

Fairly simple, if a pupil asks a question you need to answer it but remember that feedback needs to be timely and appropriate. If they are negotiating a roundabout, wait until the task is completed. Sometimes it might be appropriate to say you'll answer that at the end of the lesson. Queries are good, it means your pupil is asking questions and is thinking.

DID THE TRAINER MAINTAIN AN APPROPRIATE NON-DISCRIMINATORY MANNER THROUGHOUT THE SESSION?

We all know the obvious ones but don't fall for the less obvious ones. Typical white van man, stupid cyclists, BMW drivers never signal. (I use these as a example only and not reflection of any views) There are many more that are used that are discriminatory and the use of them just endorses views that are simply not true. Another one I will use for demonstration; busses ALWAYS pull out in front of you. Is this true? Would it not be better to ask, what might that bus do? What are you looking for? Don't make judgements on anyone or anything.

AT THE END OF THE SESSION – WAS THE PUPIL ENCOURAGED TO REFLECT ON THEIR OWN PERFORMANCE?

At the end of any driving lesson, it's important to reflect on the learning that has taken place. Not only is this of educational benefit, but it's also a chance to show your pupil that progress has been made no matter how small. It's a chance for them to go away and reflect on what they can do if they're having private practice or on what books they might need to study to look up weaknesses in knowledge. Fill in a pupil record card. Do this with the pupil getting them to reflect and tell you how well they did and if they have any concerns or questions. Do leave them looking forward to the next lesson though.

Summary

The above was a brief look at each of the standards, your trainer should cover these in more detail but there is more advice, videos and information on my free resources on my website https://dte-elite.co.uk/become-a-driving-instructor/

COACHING

The forums are full of talk about the DVSA saying driving instructors should be coaching, and coaching is what we should be using. The 'old' way of just telling someone something, does not let a pupil understand why they should do something a certain way, and they feel they just do it for a test. There is nothing complicated about coaching. Coaching by some is being made out to be a fine art. Coaching is no more than a conversation with your pupil. Albeit an engineered conversation by you, where you structure the conversation to get the pupils to the answer. So why coaching? Traditionally, teaching was about telling. The teacher told you what to do and you repeated it until you could copy what it was the teacher was doing. Driving, you checked your mirrors because your driving instructor told you to or you would fail your driving test. Pupils had it drummed into them that the examiner will be watching to see if the pupil looks at their mirror. Now, notice what I said there 'looks at their mirror'. There was no understanding of what the pupil was looking for or what to do if they saw anything. It is regrettable that I still see instructors telling pupils to look at the mirrors rather than look *into* the mirrors. Let's understand this. The Highway Code says, 'Vision and effective use.' Vision and effective use is about how the pupil reacts and deals with what is around them rather than just physically looking at a mirror. Yes, they will need to look to see but there is no point in looking if no information is seen and no necessary action taken. Question needs to be initially more about, what has been seen in the mirror than 'did you check your mirror'.

'What have you seen in your mirror?' prompts a conversation, coaching begins. As a coach, we are there to facilitate learning. To share the process and help the pupil to come to their own conclusions. The old it's my way or no way, has gone. If a pupil shows you a way to do something and it is safe, then why not stick with it. Often instructors have a set method that must be done, and they insist on them being done that way. As a novice instructor, I started to teach like that. I was very inflexible in my teaching. For example, I was told we must teach the pupil to use pull push steering methods and they must never cross their arms. Yet, in all my years driving I would often cross my arms, in fact I did so on my part two on a manoeuvre and never got a fault for it. As I started going to training events, I was hearing how examiners did not mark this unless it was a safety concern. Pupils could steer how they liked if it was safe. Now many pupils were having huge problems with this method of steering. So, I decided to try an experiment, I stopped telling them how to steer and let them get on with it. I found pupils rarely had a problem with steering. Now I understand fully the problem I was creating. Although I was telling pupils to look out the window down the road, I was also telling them about how to pull with one hand and push with the other. Even if the eyes were down the road, the brain was on the hands. The result, it seemed as if pupils could not steer. Nobody tells a child learning to ride a bike, put this hand here, when you go round a corner, pull with this hand and push with this hand. A child learns to look, and the hands follow the eyes. Isn't human nature wonderful. If they do look at the handlebars, they tend to crash! I remember my first motorbike with a full race style fairing on it. I took my first corner, looked at the fairing not turning with the handlebars and, fell off. Much to my embarrassment and the humour of the salesperson waving me off. (it was a strange concept back then)

Coaching comes from a place of, the pupil knows everything it is they need to know, and we help them with the gaps.

Rather than assuming every learner needs telling everything, we start off as though they know everything. This is a difficult concept to accept. Our natural intuition with a novice learner would be to assume we need to teach them everything. While it's probably true that we might need to teach everything, it's a frame of mind that we need to change. Sometimes it's called top-down learning. Most learners will have some knowledge even if it is just from watching parents. Open your mind and work from a place that they know everything, and you will fill in the gaps. How do we find the gaps? Questions and answers. Coaching is a more, learner centred, or 'client' centred, to use the DVSA terminology. It doesn't mean doing what the leaner (client) wants, but what the learner needs. This is a misnomer for many instructors. Asking a learner, what they want to do today is good, but we need to ascertain if it is what the learner needs. I teach and use a system called the GROW model for this.

THE GROW MODEL.

The GROW model was first mentioned in the book Coaching for performance by the late John Whitmore in (Wikipedia, n.d.)

Grow = The end point where your pupil wants to be

Reality = Where the pupil is now in terms of their goal

Options = What obstacles are in the way to stop them getting to their goal and what options are there?

Way-forward = The commitment to doing it the when, who and what.

The above I have adapted to suit the pupil but an example of how to use this on a lesson could be;

Instructor: What would you like to do today?

Pupil: We said we would do routine on approach to junctions today?

Info: So, the GOAL might be junctions but first let's look at the reality,

Instructor: What routines were we using to move off and stop?

Pupil: MSPSL and POM

Instructor: Brilliant and when we're driving, where do we normally position in the road?

Pupil: In the middle of our available space

Instructor: Correct, yes, I think junctions will be a good goal today.

Info: This was checking the reality and as it seems ok then the goal of junctions is appropriate

Instructor: What problems might we have today?

Pupil: I'm a bit worried about cars coming and who has right of way.

Instructor: That's normal, how would you like me to help you with that?

Pupil: If you could guide me and tell me at first

Instructor: Of course, no problem, what about the rest of junctions, how can I help with that?

Pupil: I quite like it when you use you diagrams to explain first.

Info: So here we are looking at the options and any obstacles.

Instructor: Ok, I will do an explanation with the diagrams, then we can spend about 20 minutes where you can have a go at some simple ones first and gradually, I will let you take more responsibility. I will especially help you with those observations at first. But if you get into difficulties, don't worry I will help you. How does that sound?

Pupil: Yes, sounds ok

Info: Here the instructor has set the way-forward, the when (20 minutes), the how (short briefing and then have a go) and the who (the instructor will give more support on the observations).

Now the above is only a very limited example to show the different stages. Often a good idea in the options stage is to use scaling. Setting a figure from 1-10 or 1-5 on how much responsibility the pupil wants, leaving the instructor with the rest. The objective is to transfer the responsibility to the pupil.

Likewise, if something develops during the lesson, a fault maybe, a mini-GROW is used. You might need to change the plan to deal with this issue. Previously we were looking at an example of routines on approach to roundabouts where the pupil displayed clutch faults. Here you would change the plan so the goal is now clutch, you would recap the clutch (Reality) and talk about what problems there are, (Options and obstacles) and how the pupil would like you to help them. Next you would decide maybe to work on the clutch for 10 minutes or so (Way-forward). The GROW model is a very useful way of completing many of the requirements of the standard check and part three test.

TELLING STORIES

When teaching subjects, it's a good idea to use stories if real scenarios cannot be found. Rather than just saying 'we are going to pull up on the right and do the reverse back two car lengths exercise', ask for scenarios where this could be useful. Going to a shop and you want to let the children out onto the pavement side, picking up an elderly relative who might not be able to walk too far or any other thing that could be useful. So, when you teach the manoeuvre, there is realism. Many instructors don't like this manoeuvre and certainly let their pupil know. This isn't promoting solid learning that will carry on for the pupil's lifetime. Asking pupils where they would find different aspects from the DVSA syllabus useful, will again give them responsibility and decision making. The good driving instructor will be inventive and will share this learning vs real life driving with the pupils. Driving lessons become a lot more fun and interesting for the pupils too. Pupils are mainly young adults and do not want to be just told when, how or if to do something.

RAPPORT IN COACHING

Coaching will not happen unless you have good rapport with your pupils. Respect who they are, share responsibility and it will come back to you. I've said it before but there are too many posts from too many instructors with the 'I've told them a thousand times before', pupils don't learn this way and if any learning does take place, it will be superficial.

What do you want as a driving instructor, safe driving for life for your pupils or superficial learning where they just pass a test?

Core competencies

Whilst we now talk more about coaching and pupil led tuition, Core competencies are still relevant and are a sound and proven way of dealing with faults. I will give a brief reminder of the functions of each here.

Fault identification or risk assessment

Without Fault identification (FI) the analysis and remedy cannot take place. Learn to give route directions to your pupil and look at them then watch your pupil through either the MSPSL or POM routine for each of the core elements. If you look for each element of Mirrors, Signal, Position, Speed and then look at where THEY look, you will see the faults. Likewise looking for the Preparation (control), Observation and the Move (Accuracy) you will see these faults. There are no other faults to spot. No matter what the subject, your only decision is which routine MSPSL (vehicle moving) or POM (stationary to moving). Practice looking for faults with these routines and you will be able to spot every fault, first time, every time.

Fault Analysis

Having spotted the fault, it's now time for the analysis (FA). This, in my opinion, is the most misunderstood of all the competencies. What you need to know first when a fault has occurred is why this fault happened. Is it a lack of knowledge, insufficient skill or down to attitude? So first ask either a 'what, where, when, how, or who' question. Try to avoid a 'why' question at this stage. The 'why' question requires more thought from your pupil and therefore may not be appropriate or well-timed yet.

Example;
Your pupil fails to check their left door mirror when turning left.
FI - You didn't check your mirror there Bob.
FA - What mirrors do we check to turn left, Bob?

Now your pupil can only give you one of two answers, a correct one or a wrong one. If they give the correct one, then a few prompts for the next junctions would suffice. A wrong answer here and we might need to pull over to look at changing the plan. So, your pupil fails to check their left door mirror when turning left:
(FI)
Instructor: You didn't check your mirror, Bob.
(FA)
Instructor: What mirrors do we check to turn left Bob?
Pupil: Oh sorry the centre and left mirror (correct)
(RA)
Instructor: Take the next road on the left and what mirrors will you use Bob

 (Prompted remedy)

Had the answer to the analysis question been wrong, then pull over and have a chat about mirrors. If there is a need to change the plan, we would use the GROW model mentioned previously.

Remedial action

You have seen here that the remedial action (RA) is directly linked to the answer to the analysis question. This makes it much easier to keep control of the lesson. However, what of the 'why' question? The Driving Instructors Handbook (2009) says 'remember to make the remedy effective and use the why question'. Here you can clearly see that the why question is part of remedy and not analysis. A pupil needs to know what it is they should do first, and then learn the why. There's little point in a pupil knocking a cyclist off a bike because they did not know what mirrors to check but did know why!! The why question is a deeper question and requires more thought so the best time to ask these are in quieter traffic moments or at the side of the road. Too many trainers try asking pupils 'why' questions, which can risk overloading a novice pupil while they try to navigate junctions etc.

> *Remember to ask the why questions when there is time and not when the pupil is busy thinking about navigating a traffic situation.*

Work your way through the levels until your pupil can complete the task independently of you. It's a good idea to use 'soft prompts' with your pupil, such as *'I will let you do your MIRRORS on your own at the next junction'*. Substitute mirrors with whatever you are letting them do on their own.

EMOTIONAL INTELLIGENCE (EQ)

Now I don't want to get too technical here or too involved and scare anyone off (Lol). Just a heads up and a bit of background. For years, people have measured intelligence by IQ. More recently it has been found that a better indicator of intelligence is by someone's emotional intelligence or EQ. I was first introduced to this at the University of East London on a coaching course. On the course we were given photographs and postcards and were asked to explain what we saw, without saying what it was using traditional methods. For example, a beach hut might be described as a small square building on the beach, made of stripey wood. It was difficult to get people to answer correctly. Then we would use emotions and say how it made us feel and the correct answers were more forthcoming. I'm feeling something soft and warm below my feet and a warm glow from the sky. I feel a nice breeze. How many are seeing a beach now? With pupils, try asking them 'how do you feel that went?' rather than 'how did that go?' Use what do you feel we need to do, rather than what do we need to do?

Another example of this is imagine a child comes home from school with a bad school report, you might feel sad about this. You might say 'you make me disappointed in this school report'. What now needs to change for this to be better? Yes, the person with the report will need to do better. Your feeling will not change until this happens. You're putting the responsibility onto the other person. What if you changed it to 'I feel disappointed with this report? Now you can choose to look for other qualities that the child has, and you can choose to feel better. EQ is used a lot now to assess candidates for job roles and University places. It's about changing the ownership to yourself. This can be a great start to a good driving instructors teaching.

DRIVING ASSESSMENT FORMS

Ensure you use some form of Driving Assessment form to record the pupil's progress. Whether you use paper or electronic is up to you, but it's important that your pupil and their parents can see how they're doing. Many disputes have been resolved easily using these and many problems can be caused by the lack of them.

MOCK TESTS

Mock test forms are also very useful 'if' they are done as proper mock tests. They're particularly useful when you can give something to your pupil that shows their test readiness. The problem is, and why many instructors don't find them useful is, they don't do it as a proper mock test. They conduct it as a normal driving lesson where they just try not to say anything. For it to work successfully, the pupil needs to feel the same stress they will on the real test. Now this is ideal if you can find another instructor who can do them for you and you for them, but I used to conduct my own mock tests and they were quite realistic.

The pupils knew that the next lesson would be a mock test, they would be told to bring their licence and theory pass certificate. I would take them to a location very near the actual test centre, to a car park to start the test. I would be equipped with a clipboard with a DVSA DL25 test marking form. Complete an eyesight test and appear official. Lead your pupil to the car just like the examiner and after the show me checks, ask them to make themselves comfortable in the car while you carry out the usual examiner checks to your vehicle. Join them and read out the examiner script about this is their practical test etc. If my pupil tried to ask questions during the test about how they should do something, I would reply with 'your instructor would have told you how this should be carried out'. The hardest part was keeping a straight face sometimes. This mock test would replicate the real test in as many details as possible. I'd use set routes and set times. At the end I would ask the pupil to switch off the engine, say I will just need a moment to check the form and give them the outcome as an examiner, I am pleased to tell you, or I am sorry to inform you etc. Then break from the official line and tell them to relax. I would ask them how they felt, and they would always say, that was hard, scary or something similar. Then I would tell them how the test will be easy compared to this. Then we would go over the faults they made. How would you do this better next time and what could you do better here, sorts of questions. Then we would very often re-drive the route but as a coaching session asking how certain things could be done better. After I would ask them, do you think you are ready for the real test, most times they would say no. Many were and we would work on the few issues and maybe do another mock test.

You can download DL25 from the internet. They can give an appraisal to your pupil of test readiness. When doing mock tests, keep them as real as possible. More information on this can be found at the DSA website under DT1. It is often a good idea to let your pupil keep this report to show their parents their readiness.

SUMMARY

The sections above on coaching etc. are just brief sections to give you a basic understanding of what is needed to be a 'good' driving instructor. Staying clear of the anti-coaching campaigners and the 'I've always done it like this' brigade. The way I teach today is far removed from when I started. Mind you, I've done a hell of a lot of CPD, far more than most. It is though, not necessary for you to follow in my exact footsteps but even if you ask yourself, 'what would a good driving instructor do?' then I am sure you will often find the answer. My driving school, 1st 4 Driving, is full of 'good' driving instructors. These driving instructors get on with delivering great driving lessons, leaving us to worry about the business side and pupils. In fact, they see the things we do as essential for them to carry out their business as good driving instructors.

Let's look at some other aspects of what being a good driving instructor involves.

NEVER JUDGE A PUPIL BY ITS COVER!

I took a phone call many years ago from a guy asking about driving lessons. His tone was, very scared. He asked me 'will I MAKE him drive on the first driving lesson.' I re-assured him he was in safe hands and not to worry. We would take it easy and if he was not ready to drive then that was OK. A couple of days later he called again to confirm, nay, plead not to make him drive on the first lessons. And the day before his lesson he called again ensuring I would not make him, or he would pay me but would not want the lesson. I have had nervous pupils before, but this was something else.

As I approached the guy's house ready for the driving lesson, I noticed a very large, tattooed guy with lots of piercings. He was massive and looked very threatening. I was early as normal for a first lesson and was preparing some notes with half an eye on this guy as he approached the car. I sheepishly opened the window at which point he asks, 'are you Dave'. 'Yes', I reply, and he announces himself as Mark, my pupil. Well, if I hadn't been sat down, I would have fallen over. He squeezes into the passenger seat and again gets me to agree not to make him drive on this lesson. You could see the perspiration coming from him. There was clearly a problem. I drove to a quiet area, not too far from other people mind you, and asked some questions. Turned out he had been involved in a bad car crash and hence his trepidations.

Gradually on about the third lesson, I got him to take the wheel and he drove a few yards. This was increased and his confidence grew. I also got to know Mark very well and he was a very nice chap indeed. Frightening to look at but a very nice man.

Mark passed his driving test on the first attempt. I used some calming methods and coaching before the test, I took him into the test centre, introduced him to an examiner pre-arranged beforehand. I still remember the look on the examiners face.

THE OTHER SIDE.

I had a small contract with a private school for young ladies. This was a very expensive and exclusive school, very prim and proper. I had taught several of the students there but one of them sticks out very well. On her first lesson, it was clear she had a bit of an attitude. She was telling me how she gets in trouble for all sorts of things. On one occasion we were overtaken by another car, and she started to speed up saying' I'm not letting this happen'. She kept wanting to drive fast and told me, when she passes her test, she will come back and show me how to drive properly.

At a set of traffic lights once, in the middle of Exeter city centre, she proceeded to try and recline the seat right back while we waited for the lights to change. She adopted a position like a racing driver. I asked her what she was doing, she explained all her friends drove like this. As the lights changed, she went to move off and stalled. She could not reach the keys from her position so pulled herself towards the keys and re-started the engine. By now the lights were back to red. Back to her racing position, I asked her 'would the position have anything to do with the stall', no she said all my friends drive like this. Lights turn green, she goes to move off and another stall. She is getting more frustrated and the cars behind are now starting to toot their horn. Eventually she puts the seat up and the move off is successful. I guide us to a particular spot and pull her over. Let's talk about what happened. We discuss about how the seating position could affect the pedal positions. We discuss about safety and vision through windows, and I ask why she wanted to drive like that. She explains it looks cool.

'Take a look to your right and tell me what you see?' I have placed us outside a very reflective shop window. So, what do we have? A girl with all the designer gear on. Designer shades and haircut. All very cool but I add 'somewhat negated by the bloody driving school logos all over the car and the big red L on the roof.' Yes, I did swear, not something I do in lessons but on this occasion, I planned it for the congruence of the lesson. She took the point.

I remember this girls first test, Gabi was the examiner (if you ever read this you might remember her). The pupil wanted to do the 5:30pm test as she had been told, all the pupils pass with this test. Now this girl to be fair had great car control skills. Her driving was good, it was her attitude that was bad. The test went well, everything fine until turning back into the test centre. Waiting for traffic to pass the pupil announces, I'm not waiting for them, and cuts right across the front. FAIL

Test 2, again she wanted the 5:30pm this time almost back at the test centre, the second to last junction and she decides to race the car to beat another to the give way line. Fail 2. Test 3, 51mph in a 40mph and I can't remember test 4 but she passed on test 5. And guess who her examiner was every time, yes Gabi as she was the only examiner doing the 5:30pm test. The pupil kept blaming the examiner and saying she was going to kick her.

After she passed, she was looking forward to mummy buying her a new car as promised. Until then she had to drive her mum's old banger (her words), a 2 year old car. When her car came one month later, mums car had so many scrapes and dents in it, mummy told her she was keeping the new car and the daughter was to have the old one. You could hear the daughters scream from Scotland.

So, my title was don't judge a pupil by their cover and first impressions don't always count. Both these pupils were challenging in their own way and both I enjoyed teaching

DAVE FOSTER MA, DIP.DI

them both, for different reasons. It's pupils like those that got me to my master's degree. It's the variety and challenges of the job I love, and I have a lot more stories like this to share.

DIFFICULT TO TEACH PUPILS.

Some years ago, I wrote an article in response to the many posts I see from driving instructors complaining about their pupils. It was headed,

THERE IS NO SUCH THING AS 'CRAP' PUPILS, JUST 'CRAP' INSTRUCTORS��

Disclaimer 1: I use the term 'crap' purely as a copy of the words used to describe pupils on social media. It's not written to cause offence or be offensive but was necessary for the point of the article

Prompted by comments (as ever) from social media, I thought I would address the issue where driving instructors talk about 'crap' pupils. Now I believe when they refer to them in this way, they mean 'pupils who do not learn as well, quick or any other adjective that does not fit 'their' norm'. But what is a norm? Certainly, in over 20 years of teaching learners, instructors, and instructor trainers I've not found it.

A pupil that learns quickly, might have found that the teaching method the instructor used fitted them. Another pupil with the same driving instructor, might not learn so well. Why is this? Well, everybody has a different way of learning. It's built into them and part of our individualism. It doesn't mean prefer as in we chose to learn in a particular way. It is pre-programmed into us as part of our DNA. I suppose, part of our make-up effects our choices in life in many other things like career, choice of clothes, choice of car maybe etc. There are 4 basic learning styles, known as VARKS and are Visual, Auditory, Read-write and Kinaesthetic. This article isn't about exploring these in any detail, this is done in my more detailed videos and articles on my Driver Training Education website that contains many free resources for driving instructors. This article highlights, why some pupils do well and some not so well and what can be done about it.

IT GETS COMPLICATED.

We need to define 'learned quickly' or any of the other adjectives used to describe pupils who, in the opinion of some driving instructors, don't do so well. What do the pupils who appeared to learn well, learn? It might be they learnt the control skill suffice to pass a driving test but might be lacking in the higher-level skills required to stay alive driving. Could you say in the long term, a pupil that passed their test first time with just 20 hours, who later suffered a horrendous crash from poor driving, learnt well? But what about that pupil who took 60 hours, passed on their 3rd attempt but went on to drive safely and crash free for life? Some might say luck played its part but as a famous golfer once said, 'the more I practice, the luckier I get.'

Disclaimer 2: Before you read the following section, I would like to point out that not all instructors are poor or fit the section below. In the section I refer to the instructors who blame their pupils for the problems and don't take the responsibility. The instructor who is active in CPD and already knows the solution to this problem, will be agreeing to the following section. They will already be teaching learners with many preferred learning styles completely satisfactory.

THE PROBLEM

The problem is, driving instructors also have an inherent 'preferred' learning style. As such when it comes to teaching, they tend to use this style as their preferred method. Anyone who doesn't learn using their style or their way, is tarnished with being 'crap'. The reality is the instructor and pupil were just not a good fit. The pupil often moves on after a period of unhappy and slow learning, to another instructor. This process repeats itself until the pupil finds an instructor they like or whose teaching methods fit. According to the DVSA, the average pupil takes around 45 hours of professional tuition and on average uses 3 instructors. Each time the pupil finds a new instructor that does not fit, they feel more and more like they are the problem and let me stress this, **the pupil is never the problem**.

THE PUPIL IS NEVER THE PROBLEM.

It is all too easy for an instructor to blame the pupil. Nobody is really monitoring the instructor. True, they have a Standard Test every 4 years or so, but the instructor will take a pupil who is a good fit, the examiner sees a one-off lesson every 4 years, where the instructor is teaching their best fit pupil. Now how we devise a test that would accommodate all pupils would be challenging!

HOW DO WE KNOW THERE IS A PROBLEM?

Well for instructors, the pupil might be learning very slowly. They might appear uninterested in your lesson or seem distracted. The pupil might particularly struggle with manoeuvres and roundabouts. The pupil will often keep cancelling lessons with what might seem like weak excuses.

As the pupil, you will feel you're not making progress and don't enjoy your driving lessons. You will be looking for any excuse to cancel. Often you will feel you are only turning up for fear the instructor will charge you anyway for the lesson. You will feel like you will never learn, and you are a problem. Let me say this again **THE PUPIL IS NEVER THE PROBLEM.** Does this feel like you?

THE SOLUTION

Well for the pupil there are 2 solutions.

1. Keep trying driving instructors until you find one who fits your learning style. This is an expensive and demoralising way but often there is little choice.
2. Find a driving instructor who doesn't have a one size fits all teaching style. Ask many of your friends about their instructor and try to find a few people learning with one instructor. Choose different friends. By 'different' I mean friends who have different hobbies, lessons, or jobs. Look for the arty friends and the ones into maths. Look for ones who play musical instruments and the one who like to sit and read. If you find an instructor who all these pupils seem to learn well with, chances are they use a variety of teaching methods to suit each learner.

For the instructor there are 2 solutions.

1. Carry on as you are, cherry pick the pupils that are your perfect fit. Although, you are limiting your client base and not really challenging yourself!
2. Learn about VARKS and how to identify the different types of learners. Learn how to change your style of learning to fit each learner. Learn how so much more rewarding it is to look at EVERY pupil as a success and a rewarding experience. Enjoy more pupils because of it and enjoy your job. Oh, and see far fewer cancelled lessons too, without threatening charges.

MY CONCLUSIONS ON THIS SUBJECT ARE.

All instructors are encouraged by the DVSA, the governing body, to use a variety of teaching styles and methods. Long gone are the days when in school, the teacher just wrote out a load of writing on a board and told pupils to just copy it. Today's driving instructors have all the resources open to them to learn modern forward-thinking methods and fortunately, those that are not moving forward are becoming a thing of the past and will eventually meet the same fate as the dinosaurs.

HOW TO UNDERSTAND HOW TO TEACH ANYTHING

A question that I am asked a lot is, how do I teach _____ or how do I teach _____. Fill in the space with any subject because I have been asked probably how to teach any of them.

TODAY I AM GOING
TO SHARE A SECRET!

You are going to find out the secret for yourself.

It's something that will help your training massively and you will suddenly understand how to teach so many things you did not know possible.

A LITTLE BACKGROUND FIRST.

Let me remind you of some background information as to where this secret comes from. I was a full time employed instructor trainer for many years, previously I was an instructor trainer for the AA and later I was a Director of Training for a medium sized driving school, suffice to say I have trained hundreds. Then I was rescuing many instructors who had failed multiple attempts at part three. I have taken many professional qualifications and used my background to help with my master's degree in Driver Training Education. So, suffice to say I know about this subject.

I have talked many times about the fact many trainees simply fail to look in the right place but today I am talking about another secret. The secret many trainers will not tell you. Why? Because they don't understand it themselves? Maybe. Because they find it easier to just not teach this? Maybe. But it's something I see time and time again and one of the most unanswered questions on any social media platform.

So, I will give you an insight into how many of my successful trainees discovered this.

YOU ARE NOT ALONE.

Nearly every time I met someone for rescue work, I would ask them to teach me the same subject. To emerge from junctions. Now apart from the fact almost every time nobody ever actually started teaching from the off, rather let me mess up first, the secret was that when it came to teaching ANYTHING I would be met with 'how do I teach that?' And my reply was always, 'what do you do?' This would be met with something like 'I just do it' or' I just know 'etc. and this is the massive secret. Inside you, yes everyone is the secret on how to teach any subject, but you must analyse completely what YOU DO. This will seem very difficult at first, if not impossible but when you unlock the secret on how YOU precisely do anything, you have your answer. No more asking on Facebook 'how do I teach the bay park?' or 'how do I get the pupil to stay away from parked cars?' or any of the other million questions in the same vein.

One of the things I used to do was, in the coffee shop, I would ask a trainee to write down the steps to make a cup of coffee. (Anyone who is reading this and has done this with me will be laughing already) Now this sounds like a simple task, but it never works. I would then try to follow their written instructions.

Things like:

Put a spoon of coffee in (but not saying what size spoon)

Put in water (but not saying allow enough room for milk)

Add water (but not saying bring to boil)

Etc.

However, here is the point of this exercise, now I would ask them to do it again and nearly always it would be almost perfect. They had learnt how to extract the information hidden inside them. The same goes for everything you teach. You will need to refine everything of course but when you start doing this, amazingly you will experience the ability to teach better. We used to do the cup of coffee exercise with The Instructor College, but they missed the important second stage where you show the trainee how much better they can get it when they understand the detail required. They used to stop after the first attempt leaving the trainee feeling very silly. But then that's how many trainers used to train, you have a go, get it wrong, look stupid and next week you look stupid doing a completely new subject.

SO WHY NOT JUST USE EVERYONE ELSE'S SYSTEM?

Many trainees want or expect someone to give them fixes to every problem, to give them ways of doing everything. This might seem like an easy way to training but it's superficial and often the 'tricks' don't work. Like a learner learning the Highway Code rules by multiple choice only, those instructors will fall down later. There are unfortunately many schools and trainers who are still prepared to teach this method. Let's face it, it's easier for the trainer too but trust me, learn the simple secret on how you do everything, and every single driving fault, technique and methods is open to you instantly.

Many times, I would be told something like, to get a learner to turn at the right point, make them line the T up from the white lines level with the door mirror. (you'll know the one) Back in the old day, the examiner would role play, and the trainee would find the examiner couldn't do this. I would ask the trainee, 'Do you do this when driving?' no, of course not, 'Have you ever tried it?' no 'go on then let's try it' and guess what? They couldn't do it that way. Back to my question 'what do you do?' umm rinse and repeat... There are lots of them out there. But remember not everyone learns the same way, it's good to have other ways but not the stock 'my trainer told me to do this'. I suppose a better question on any forum would be 'what do other instructors actually do?' when driving rather than 'what do they teach?'

DO I USE REFERENCE POINTS WHEN TEACHING?

Well yes, I do sometimes, because I use them when driving. But I know that every pupil is a different size so I encourage them to find their own reference, guiding them to where they might be found. I have also found pupils give me new ways they do things and have taken them on board. If it works, it works. I use what I do as a starting point and build and adapt with the pupil.

COACHING AND 'WHAT I DO'.

Now this doesn't mean you must tell every pupil to do what you do, far from it. But pupils will require help, and this is where your knowledge comes in. If you know the precise steps to make something work, then you are 90% of the way there to helping the pupil. If you find the correct position in the road by looking far into the distance and lining up behind a car that you can see is in the correct position, you could ask your pupil who was struggling, 'where are you looking?' or 'what do you think of the car in fronts position?' as an example of course, I'm not going to tell you what to do ��.

HOW DOES YOUR PART TWO FIT IN?

During your part two, you drove a perfect or near perfect drive. You did that your way and it worked. Part three is about transferring that skill to the pupil. Why give them Fred's from Twitters way or Wendy from Facebook? (Fred and Wendy are fictitious names used for the writing of this article and have no bearing on anyone who could be called Fred or Wendy). Use the system method, the way you did your part two as a basis. It might be harder than asking someone else, but the results are better and once you find one way, you discover how to do all the other things.

It's not easy at first.

At first it might seem difficult but ultimately it will open up new ideas and you'll realise you did have the knowledge inside you all along. That's what true coaching is, bringing out the knowledge and skills that already exist within.

STRUCTURED THEORY TRAINING

As of February 2012. The DVSA removed the questions bank of theory questions from the public domain. This is a good idea as it will encourage learners to learn correctly. There is much controversy over this and some criticism for learning challenged groups. Experienced instructors will know how a pupil can come to you having passed a theory test and have no understanding or application of it on the road. Good driving instructors will incorporate the theory in with the driving lessons. Using every opportunity to ask pupils, 'what does the Highway Code say about this' etc. All too often I see driving instructors who seem to separate the theory as something they are not responsible to teach. Posts on forums saying how they don't teach the theory and how pupils are so 'stupid' not learning it. To fully understand any subject, practical application needs to happen. It's bad enough that this doesn't happen in part one for driving instructors. As an instructor, you have ample opportunity to bring both theory and practical together and it can be a fun and enjoyable experience for both instructor and pupil alike. Teaching practical application sets your pupils up for situations that they might not come across and give them the background knowledge to deal with it.

BOOKING DRIVING TESTS

As previously mentioned, I would always book the pupils test for them, only this morning I took a phone call from an instructor who was sat outside a very closed and locked up test centre with their pupil. Apparently, the pupil had booked the test, and the instructor has not seen sight of the confirmation. Now they don't know what to do and I suspect it's the pupil who has the wrong date. It could be another day soon when the instructor is unable to help, or outside the cancellation period for the DVSA. Now it could be argued that it is the pupil's responsibility and fault but who is the professional, who will get any negative backlash? This is so easily avoided and really shouldn't happen.

PREPARING YOUR PUPILS FOR TEST DAY

Test day for pupils brings a whole lot of new emotions and in many cases, you will need to make allowances and extra precautions. There are many things driving instructors do inadvertently that help pupils prepare to FAIL a driving test. Many I have talked about before such as not using standard route direction, what an instructor wears or continuing giving instruction right up to test day. This is the day your pupils will be on their own, making the decisions themselves and this should not be the first day they have had to make all the decisions on their own. They need to be well practiced in driving without instruction and making all the decisions themselves. If they are not, it is no wonder that test nerves are cited as the most popular reason for pupils failing their test. Think about it, not only would that be the first day they have had to make all the decisions but today they must do it with a stranger sitting next to them. See my point! So, there is a lot you can do to help with this.

There are many basic things that the good driving instructor will ensure happen. Ensure you allow adequate time to get your pupil to the test. Most instructors do a one-hour lesson before but if your test centre is some distance away, more time may be required. On the lesson before the test, ensure your pupil knows what they must bring and what time you will pick them up. Your car should be clean anyway but ensure it is very clean inside and out. When you meet the pupil on the day, the first thing to do is check they have all the paperwork before you drive off. Going over all the show me tell me checks before you move off is a good idea too. This way if there's a problem, you can sort it out now and if something does happen on the journey to the test centre (like a bulb blowing for example) at least your pupil knows it must've happened on the journey. Remember you're responsible if anything goes wrong with your car for the test. You could end up paying for the test and several lessons free for the sake of a bulb failure.

WHAT THE PUPIL MUST BRING

For all types of tests

They should take:

- Their Driving Licence
- Their theory test pass certificate (or confirmation) if they are not exempt.
- Some confirmation of the test

Now I know there are many who say there is no need to take the theory test certificate or confirmation, but it expressly says so on the confirmation email. In 20 years, my pupils have been asked twice for it due to a computer problem with the examiners. A good driving instructor would ensure their pupil never had that added stress of an examiner asking for it, minutes before their driving test.

To set the scene of test days for you, as I picked up my pupil for test, the first thing I asked for was the paperwork. This I checked and placed into my door pocket, checking it went in and not slipped out. Show me tell me checks would be done on the vehicle and a very relaxed driver would appear. If the pupil smoked, then this was the only lesson I would ask if they wanted a smoke before the test. This would happen down the road from the test centre and well away from the car. At the test centre, arriving 9 minutes before the test, I asked them if they wanted the toilet, I took the keys, (I never locked the car) while they went to the toilet. With their paperwork, I would remove anything from the plastic wallet and stack it in order plastic photo licence, paper part of licence, theory test certificate then test confirmation. These were placed down on the table in front of us ready for the examiner. The pupil was then given the keys as they came back to the waiting room and sat down. So why did I do it all like this? Well over the years I have seen many things happen. Pupils give examiners their licence still in the plastic folder, only to be handed it back asking for it to be removed. You could see the pupils getting flustered or thinking they were stupid. I know we could argue they aren't, but it is at this moment we have little control, and the pupil feels small. Also, the examiners knew I sorted out my pupils properly and it set the tone for the test. Examiners know if you get the basics right, the rest will follow. Today, we don't have plastic wallets or paper counterparts, but the principle is the same. Look for the little things that can cause your pupil to worry and eliminate them. I often used to have a little light-hearted joke with one of the senior examiners as they came down to collect their pupil for test. He like me wore comedy ties, one of us would often say to the other, 'did you get that for Christmas' or something similar, adding 'you wouldn't buy it'. This was done to relax the pupils and see that the examiners are human. There are instructors in the test centre who almost snarl when they see the examiners. How must the more sensitive pupils feel seeing this?

WHAT CAR IS NEEDED FOR A CAR DRIVING TEST

Pupils do not have to take a driving test in a driving school car. If they feel comfortable and well-practiced, there is no reason why they couldn't take it in their own car or someone else's. But there are some basics they might need to know. As to what can be used for the driving test.

The car or van you use for your test must be:

- A four-wheeled vehicle of no more than 3,500 kilograms (kg) maximum authorised mass (MAM)
- Capable of a speed of at least 62.5 miles per hour (mph) or 100 kilometers per hour (km/h)
- Fitted with a speedometer that measures speed in mph visible to the examiner
- Displaying L-plates ('L' or 'D' plates in Wales) on the front and rear, but not interfering with the driver's or examiner's view
- A smoke-free environment

The vehicle must also be fitted with:

- A seatbelt for the examiner
- A passenger head restraint – it doesn't need to be adjustable but must be an integral part of the seat - 'slip on' types aren't allowed.
- An interior mirror for the examiner's use

The vehicle must be legal and roadworthy and have no warning lights showing - for example, the airbag warning light.

You will not be asked to show your insurance or MOT but will sign a declaration at the beginning of the test to confirm this is all ok. In these post COVID times, the car needs to be very clean inside and out and examiners might open a couple of windows for ventilation.

TEST DAY NERVES

I have mentioned that driving test nerves are by far the most cited reason for pupils failing their driving test. The good driving instructors will do things to help overcome most of these causes for nerves. Driving test nerves can only be overcome by having plenty of practice. Not practice the same as driving lessons where the instructor keeps telling or asking questions but more independent practice where the pupil is able to just drive independently, where they get used to making ALL the decisions and choices in their driving. Your own chat should have nothing to do with driving but getting the pupil used to real driving. Remember, this is not a lesson where you simply talk about stuff, but a lesson where you are deliberately talking about stuff (non-driving related) to achieve an independent driver. I spoke about this earlier but don't forget, around six weeks before a test, ask your pupil 'if your test was today, what would you be worried about'. Picture this; imagine your pupil wasn't confident in the reverse park or a reverse to the left or maybe there is a particular roundabout in your town they don't like, or a road junction or hill start. Chances are, they may not feel confident in one or more of the above reasons. Now imagine they're at the test centre waiting to do the test; what are they going to be thinking about? Yes, they will be worried about the route the examiner is taking and will be hoping they don't get those things they are worried about. What are their chances? How will they feel in this situation? True, they may not get those things, but they will still worry and probably mess up the things they are good at because they're not concentrating.

The only sure way to pass a test and cure nerves is

to ensure that they have enough professional lessons and additional practice to ensure that they are fully confident in all manoeuvres.

There are some other basics often overlooked. If they wear glasses or contact lenses, make sure they take them. Often pupils leave them off for vanity or other reasons. As said before, make sure they have both parts of their driving licence, theory test pass certificate and your appointment letter with you (if applicable). Often pupils will ask you 'what should they wear for their driving test?' Tell them to wear appropriate and comfortable clothing; take off any thick coats before the test as they might make them feel uncomfortable. An examiner is not marking them on the latest designer wear. I had a pupil who used to turn up for lessons with those trousers halfway down their bum. He also wore a thick chain as a belt. Every lesson he would take some time trying to get comfortable, until I asked him what he could do to avoid this ritual every time he got in the car. Next lesson the trousers were on normally (pulled up). However, on test day he turns up with the trousers down round his bum again showing most of his pants. As he walked out the test centre, I can still see the examiner walk behind then look back to me and shrug his shoulders with that 'what on earth!' look. In the car they get and sure enough, the ritual of him trying to get comfortable began, 2 minutes later the door opens, the pupil gets out and pulls his trousers up properly. The examiner was shaking his head in disbelief. As with all lessons, pupils should wear clothes that make them feel comfortable and that goes for footwear too. New trainers are not always a good idea and NOT flip flops!

The debate about sunglasses pops up a lot with driving instructors as to whether pupils are allowed to wear them. Of course, they are. Instructors worry about the examiner seeing them check a mirror but remember, the examiner looks for the reactions to the following traffic rather than the mirror check itself. A pupil can look at the mirror all they want but if they don't make effective use of the mirrors, it will end badly. Your pupil might find it useful to take some water with them. It's ok to ask the examiner if they can stop for a few moments to calm themselves.

You should aim to arrive between 5 to 10 minutes before the test is due to start. Don't arrive earlier than ten minutes before, you may get in the way of other tests returning and the examiner won't like that. Tell them to keep calm. If they don't understand what the examiner has asked them to do, just politely ask them to repeat the instruction. If they go the wrong way, tell them not to worry, they are not being tested on their ability to follow directions just that they drive safely. If they make a mistake, tell them not to give up, just do it again correctly. Many pupils have thought they'd failed when in fact they hadn't, examiners look at some faults and think although it was a fault, it didn't matter and sometimes don't even record it. If they haven't done anything terribly wrong or dangerous, they can still pass.

Talk to your pupils about the possibility of a second supervising examiner sitting in on the test too. It is good practice to let your pupils know this in case it happens and throws them. This is nothing for the pupil to worry about and ensure standardisation of test marking etc.

THE DEBRIEF

When the driving test has ended, if you didn't go with your pupil on your test, you should at least listen to the debrief. This is so you can listen to the result and feedback with your pupil. The examiner will say whether they passed or failed and will explain how their driving was during the test. They will also give helpful feedback about how eco-efficient their driving was. This is a very important chance for a good instructor to listen and learn about what else they can be doing.

IF YOUR PUPIL FAILS

I always found that one of the hardest drives with a pupil was that drive home if they failed. You will both feel disappointed. But there are things you can do to turn it into something positive. The most important thing is to never blame the examiner, never blame the route, and never blame the day or time. The only reason your pupil failed was because they did something wrong that didn't meet the required standard. Now don't go telling them that directly, rather ask them what they would do differently next time. Don't dwell on it too much but let them know you will work on this together next lesson. Always drive them home, their emotions will be all over the place. Tell them you will book their next test later today for them for a date as soon as possible. Confirm their next driving lesson. On the next driving lesson, I used to re-visit the test route with them. Remember, let them make the decisions and if there were faults from the test, ask what could you do differently? Work on these small issues until they are fully independent. If the re-test is some time ahead, it might be worth setting up a different lesson schedule such as 2-hours every two weeks. Often the pupil will still want and ask for weekly lessons, this often feels unnecessary, but we're doing what we can to make the pupil feel confident. Use the time to show how independent they really are.

I think it's wise to talk about why we should not blame the examiner, quotas, the route, or next doors cat. A common thing amongst driving instructors is to blame the examiner. Examiners are tested regularly to ensure that they all mark to a consistent standard. I know there appears to be the odd inconsistency, but no examiner would be able to do their own thing for too long. Let's look at this from a pupil's point of view. A driving instructor blames a certain examiner, the pupil books another test and on the next test, who should call their name, yes, the same examiner. How is your pupil's confidence right now? Rock bottom if you've said anything like 'they fail everybody'. Similarly, quotas or days of weeks/times. More importantly you are taking away ownership of the fault from the pupil. A pupil can do nothing about an examiner, the day of week, the time, the route, or anything else an instructor blame. But a pupil can do something about it if they take responsibility if it was their fault. Read back on my section on emotional intelligence. If your pupil has done more work towards the next test, they will feel in a better place to pass it. This also sets the tone for the rest of their driving after they pass. It is the essence of good driving, taking ownership of their mistakes. In fact, it's not a bad moral for life in general. If you're one of the driving instructors who believe it was the examiner's fault, then why are you giving your pupil more lessons? Surely you should just book another test until they get a different examiner!

WHEN YOUR PUPILS PASS

Drive them home. They probably want to text or call people and will be excited and emotional and not really in the best frame of mind to drive. If their photo card driving licence was issued after 1 March 2004, they'll be given the option to have their full licence issued electronically. The examiner will take the licence off them, scan the details, and send them electronically to DVLA. They'll be given a pass certificate, as proof of passing, and DVLA will send the full licence to them within four weeks of passing their practical test.

TRAINEE LICENCE SCHEME

Once upon a time when the part three test was role play, all you had to do was learn and rehearse 10 pre-set tests. Today you deliver a real driving lesson to a real pupil, and this takes a lot of practice. Whilst it's suggested you can take a family member or friend; I have seen this go wrong too many times. The trainee licence scheme is a way to practice with real pupils carrying out real lessons. Just like preparing for the learner test, trainee driving instructors need to practice and gain real life experience so they can deliver every aspect of driving lessons. Now the trainee licence has been criticised many times by driving instructors. My master's degree research looked specifically at the trainee licence scheme and how similar it is to many other models. The scheme is, in effect, what's known as a reflective practice model. This is one where you practice with supervision, gradually decreasing as you gain confidence. It's used by doctors, teachers, and many other professions without criticism. I've often wondered how people would feel having an operation by a doctor who had only ever read the textbooks or done the classroom theory! Done right, the trainee licence scheme works well. It gives the trainee a greater choice of pupils to take for their test and gives the trainee a greater understanding of what can happen.

TRAINEE INSTRUCTORS VALUABLE ADVICE;

Remember that the trainee licence is primarily given so you can learn and prepare for the qualification as a driving instructor. Yes, you're allowed to earn money but never lose sight of the main reason. Every lesson given should be reflected on as to what went well, what didn't go so well and what you need to do to improve. Too many trainee instructors go about it as just earning money and forgetting the all-important fact.

Deliver EVERY driving lesson as if it's your part three test. Almost every trainee I've ever sat in on for the first time, they don't set any real objectives. Rather they tend to just appear to go for a drive with a pupil, fault correcting as they go along. Every lesson needs to be goal focused, have a goal in mind for each lesson. Use the GROW model which I spoke of earlier, get into the good habit right from lesson one. Spend time after each lesson reflecting on the points mentioned above and don't get into bad habits. Speak with your trainer regularly. Ensure you make your training sessions with your trainer the priority. I often get trainees tell me; they are too busy to do training. Without following this advice, you'll be on a slippery road to bad tuition and it's harder to break bad habits later. Remember, good teaching isn't difficult and is easier than bad teaching, but you'll need to get into the habits of setting goals, recapping, and reflecting. Agree with your pupil what you will do today (Goal), talking about what has happened or what could happen (recapping), and thinking about how it could be done differently (Reflecting).

The good instructor trainer will work with you and help you chose the best pupil for your test. They will discuss your potential plan for the test with you.

There are a few legal requirements you need to remember when on a trainee licence.

You are responsible for the use of your licence. You must not advertise yourself as if you were a fully qualified instructor. Your trainee licence shows the name and address of your training establishment, and you can only give instruction from there. You aren't allowed to work independently from your supervisor, e.g. by setting up your own school. Ensure you receive the required amount of supervision or additional training while your licence is still valid. Ensuring you receive this training is your responsibility. You must continue to ensure you're a 'fit and proper' person. So, keep out of trouble. You must display the licence on the nearside edge of the front windscreen of your car whilst you're giving instruction.

When you pass
Once you have passed the third and final part of the Approved Driving Instructor (ADI) qualifying examination, you can apply to join the ADI Register.
You must apply to join the Approved Driving Instructor (ADI) Register within one year of passing the ADI part three test of instructional ability. The easiest way to apply is online and you can do this by following the link here Apply for your ADI licence on-line if you are viewing this electronically. Otherwise go to the business link website and search for applying for your ADI licence on-line.

If you don't, your qualification will become invalid, and you'll have to restart the qualification process with the part one theory test.

Your certificate must be displayed on the nearside edge of the front windscreen of your car while you give instruction. You're also encouraged to display your certificate while your pupils are taking their tests. The police and authorised officers of the Department for Transport may ask you to show your certificate on demand.

If you fail

If you fail your first or second attempt at the ADI part three test, you must provide evidence that you have taken five hours additional training at the time of your next attempt, otherwise your trainee licence may be revoked. This can simply be a signed letter confirming your additional five hours from your trainer. In the unlikely event that you were to fail all three, DO NOT tell your pupils you have failed and can no longer teach them!! This can lead you open to parents demanding their money back from you as they feel they have been cheated. My advice would be to say you've given up for personal reasons. It's hoped that this is only a temporary halt in your training, and a good driving school will endeavour to help you out so you can re-start your training and come around again. Always try to pace your part three tests to maximise your licence and so that if you're taking a third and final, it's as close to your two-year expiry date as possible so you can be back on the road again and teaching as soon as possible. You may still be able to re-take your previous pupils upon returning and at the very least their friends. So be careful what you tell them if you did fail all three tests.

Coming round again

Coming around again is, IF you failed the complete process by failing 3 part three tests or 3 part two tests, then you start the whole process again. Firstly, I want to add that it's a very big IF, if you are with my driving school, or for that matter any training school who knows about the training properly. It does happen for many reasons. Don't be despondent or give up. I know a trainer who failed multiple times and is now a top grade ORDIT instructor. Failing can only make you stronger. Throughout this book, I have tried to show how easy this can be, and it's only made complicated by poor training. Whilst I personally have trained people who have failed three attempts and have come around again, nobody I have trained has been in this situation if they followed the training. If you do find yourself in this temporary position, here is some advice following.

If you had failed and your two years are up, you need to retake all three parts again. In theory it shouldn't take you too long for your part one theory and HPT test. This can be completed in the first week. Also, theoretically your part two driving test should be simple too and not require too much if any training. So, depending on test availability you can be back to part three in weeks! You'll still need to complete your initial 40-hour part three training if you wanted to go back on a trainee licence, but you can be up and running back on your trainee licence very quickly and we have helped quite a few instructors from other schools to do just this. In fact, I know of two trainers who are now ORDIT qualified who did just that!

To sum up;

- *Don't tell your learners you've failed any part three tests.*
- If you were unfortunate enough to fail all three attempts at part three, then it's possible to have you back on the road and learning again quite quickly.
- A good driving school will help you back on the road again as much as they can.

YOUR CONTINUING PROFESSIONAL DEVELOPMENT (CPD)

WHAT IS CPD?

Once you're qualified as a driving instructor, your training should never stop. Training can take many forms and could be simply reflecting on how you can do things better or attending the many training courses that are springing up. I'm a little worried as to some of these courses. Some seem to have no substance of professional qualification behind them. There has been much talk and confusion as to what is CPD. CPD stands for Continuing Professional Development and as such needs to be 'continuing'. Simply attending any course whether it's fleet, NVQ or any seminar or workshop won't count as CPD unless you can evidence what it is you learnt from it. If you attend a course and don't learn anything from it, then it's not Professional Development. It's not the bright shiny certificate you get at the end but the way you evidence and reflect on what you have learnt. Now all this may sound complicated, but it really isn't. The DSA have downloads of forms you can record your CPD on

Your CPD is evidenced in the following way;

- State the competency the CPD is linked too. This framework is shown on the following page
- Make a summary of what you learnt
- Write out the possible application(s) of what was learned and impact on career/business
- List any future development/activities
- Review later to ask yourself what went well and what you could do to improve it.

Continuing Professional Development (CPD)

Competence Framework
(Based on work carried out by Red Scientific 2005)

Monitoring & Assessment:
- Evaluation of road & traffic conditions to drive trainee's actions.
- Supervision of trainee's driving
- Directing trainee's in specific actions & manoeuvres.
- Monitoring of trainee's progress
- Provision of feedback to trainees.
- Recording of trainee's achievement.
- Supervision of trainee's through assessment
- Directing trainee's future development & training.
- Evaluation of own teaching performance

Strategy & Planning:
- Strategy & planning
- Lesson delivery
- Instructor development

Instruction Delivery:
- Demonstration of driving skills & methods
- Coaching of driving skills & methods

Driving Knowledge:
- Road & traffic knowledge
- Vehicle knowledge

Driving Skills:
- Vehicle handling ability
- Awareness of driving situation

Driving Abilities:
- Sensory perception
- Cognitive abilities
- Physical movement & coordination.

Communication Skills:
- Appropriateness
- Watching
- Speaking
- Listening
- Writing / Drawing
- Non-verbal communication
- Special needs training

Personal Characteristics:
- Attitude
- Awareness
- Instruction

Business Practice:
- Monitoring & controlling resources
- Record keeping
- Health, safety & welfare
- Relationships with trainees, customers & the general public

Business Development:
- Sales & marketing
- Staff recruitment
- Vehicle selection

NOTES:

Competency framework

For CPD to count you must also use it. I've met many instructors who have obtained a fleet qualification and haven't used it. This makes the qualification not 'continuing' and leaves the holder with a problem on a Standards test as they have no experience of teaching the fleet corporate driver. Imagine trying to do an ordinary Standards test when you haven't been teaching learners for a couple of years!!

Plan your CPD so you know what you'll do with it when you've obtained it. Know where you are going to use it and what you're going to use it for.

CPD must have value to you by enhancing your teaching or your income.

Evidencing

Keep a folder with all your records in and ensure you complete them after each course of CPD. Filling them in as soon after the course as possible would be wise, so that it's fresh in your mind. Try to claim for as much as you can too, if you can find something about a competency you've learned, you can claim credit for it. Try to make a date each year when you will plan your CPD activities for that year and set a review date. This is a date with yourself to review your CPD or could be someone else.

It's worth pointing out that if you decide to go for a degree with Middlesex University, all this evidence can be used to count towards your degree in something called Recognition of Accredited Learning (RAL) portfolio. These credits can amount to as much as 240 credit points towards a 360-credit point BA (Hons) degree. That means you may have completed as much as two thirds of a degree without doing anything more than your normal CPD studies.

CHAPTER 7:
BUILDING YOUR OWN
DRIVING SCHOOL

I hesitated to write this chapter, after all it's what I now do, run my own driving school. So why would I tell other driving instructors how to do it? Well, I'm not going into the tiny detail, that would be another book! But I decided to sketch out the basics so driving instructors have at least an outline of what's involved. Remember, all the way through this book I'm all about helping driving instructors become 'good' driving instructors and helping those that would otherwise fail. Running your own driving school can be very rewarding. More than the financial side, that I will talk about later, but the rewards seeing new driving instructors take to the roads and the satisfied feeling I have this year, as I reflect on the changes I made to my own driving school last year. I'm very proud of all my driving instructors working for my school, something I couldn't have said this time last year. Why? I will try to explain next.

Setting up a driving school changes the goal posts completely. Assuming you're a good instructor who likes to teach well and give great customer service, I would assume you want the same for your driving school. This all changes the moment you become a driving school with more than one driving instructor. Very few driving instructors will think like you. In my time I've found a few will have their own agenda and ideas.

When there are problems (and there will be), you'll have to deal with the complaints. Believe me, even your nicest instructor who you'd never believe would have a complaint, will at some point. By the time it gets to you, the pupil or more likely the parents will have exhausted communication with the instructor and will be coming to you to resolve whatever it is. Now to be fair, mum and dad or whoever is calling you will only have had their kins version. I've had a few novice staff who've heard a complaint for the first time and started to take the side of the parent, 'do you know what our instructor x has done?'. Wait until you've heard instructor x version first, the truth always lies in the middle. However, this aside, your business takes on a new dimension. Now your customer is your driving instructor, and the pupils are secondary, well to a degree. Let me give an example, a complaint about one of my longest serving instructors. An instructor who never gets complaints and is very popular with hundreds of great reviews. A parent calls because this instructor won't teach their pupil to drive. They're demanding not only their money back but a further 10 hours for compensation. They say they accept the instructor was ill with COVID but why are they chasing the instructor. Speaking with the instructor it seems the parents forgot to mention the times the instructor turned up and the pupil wasn't there. Or the fact that the pupil themselves caught COVID and was unavailable for lessons for some time. Add to the mix that this was over Christmas and new year, a new story appears. The parents want a new instructor but of course, we don't currently have anyone else available. Or the pupil and instructor who turned up at the wrong test centre. Despite the fact the pupil was sent a copy of the test booking stating the test centre and the instructor's diary says the correct test centre, the pupil expects the school to pay for the new driving test. Yes, it's been a busy few days for complaints!! These happen and they're normally easily resolved. But harder are the ones where the pupils complain about their driving instructor. When you start your driving school, occasionally you will need to deal with this sort of thing.

Your instructors are your fee-paying customers and pupils are how they earn their money. Your business structure needs to change to find out what it is you need, to attract driving instructors, but at the same time pupils. Up to now, we assume pupils come to you because they want YOU to teach them. They've been recommended or have heard about your calm manner, pass rate or whatever. Now your driving school needs to attract pupils for different reasons.

INSTRUCTOR RECRUITMENT

Most driving instructors at some point, dream of setting up their own driving school but there are many aspects to running a multi car driving school. You'll need to recruit instructors and generate pupils, lots of pupils. Now you might get by with 20, 30, or 40 pupils a year yourself but there's something quite odd about instructors that work for your driving school. Very often they seem to... well, eat pupils. We use this term jokingly in the office for an instructor that seems to need an unusual number of pupils. We all lose the odd pupil but the instructors I'm talking about lose 2 out of 3. They'll blame an offer or the pupils 'having lesson breaks' or the pupil is undecided or some other excuse. Yes, it happens to us occasionally, but we are talking 2 out of 3 pupils, maybe more. These instructors are a drain on resources and furthermore, there are lots of pupils saying not so good things about your driving school. We do offer training and advice for these instructors but first, you must get them to accept that they're the problem. I've said earlier, pupils will leave an instructor for a variety of reasons, not making progress, instructor unreliable, instructor not making them feel comfortable, instructor shouting and a few more, yet instructors never site these reasons as to why the pupil leaves. They will blame the pupil, the offer, the quality of the pupil etc. It's one of the most difficult parts of the business. If a driving instructor wants to join your driving school, you need to ask yourself why. Now there are good ones out there, some very good. Most of my instructors come from people I have trained. But sometimes you get an instructor who's a good instructor but couldn't or doesn't want to, do all the business side. Sometimes they have tried to set up their own driving school and it's not worked out as well as they'd hoped. These are often very good instructors who, rather than give up and leave the professions, stayed but looked for a good driving school to work with. Sometimes, like me, instructors join a driving school for the training and security and can develop their own teaching skills. Be cautious of the instructor who comes to you struggling for work though. In my early days I found myself taking on any driving instructor. I was building a driving school and if they were willing to join, I was happy. But 2 things happened. I stopped enjoying the driving school as the complaints were coming in thick and fast and we were getting bad Google reviews. Some complaints ended up going to the DVSA due to their serious nature. Not a good time. I had to sit down and ask myself, what was my original intention of my driving school, what did I want. I had set myself up all my career as top of my field. I called my driving school 1st 4 Driving, because I wanted to be just that. But I had fallen for the trap that so many schools do, build no matter what the cost. Well, I took a brave move, and cleaned the driving school up. Any new recruits are interviewed by me and some haven't made the grade. It's a hard decision when you must meet a wages bill at the end of every month. I will say now though it was worth it and I'm back building the driving school I wanted. Oh, and the complaints have stopped too.

One of the first things you will need when setting up your own driving school is to decide what you stand for. What is your Unique Selling Point (USP). Now stop for a moment and think of one, go no further in this book until you've given brief thought as to what your USP could be. Done it? I bet it's something to do with pupils! Remember you're a driving school now, what is the USP for your future driving instructors.

DO I NEED A WEBSITE?

There will be instructors who will tell you that you don't. But I'll tell you that you most definitely do. A website is yours; you have control of it. Unlike Facebook or any other type of social networking, you have total control. Only yesterday I saw a post from a driving school who have lost all their Facebook reviews and have been blocked by Facebook. They have no idea why and will struggle to get it back. I know, as this happened to me. I had built a good community on my DTE platform for training. Reviews, likes and followers and overnight, Facebook pulled the plug. After endless hours, then weeks and even months of talking to their automated robots, we had to give up, gone and lost forever. The post I was referring to yesterday has others telling a similar story about how their Facebook or Google reviews got removed.

One of my favourite stories about instructors who kept telling everyone that all you need is Facebook, the 2 most prolific supporters, have now left the industry. But your own website is an evergreen asset, something that will continue to build and grow, and you can change as the market changes. A website can be a platform for things like your terms and conditions, payment methods and all manner of things. Currently, a company that doesn't have a website, and checkable information could be seen as, well not a company.

If you're still happy to think you don't need a website, are you happy that your pupils will most definitely be looking for you on the internet? Will you be happy that they won't see you, but they will see your competitors? Your competitors know this and will have tempting offers and testimonials to tempt them away. You see, a website is a place to also showcase your testimonials and pupil reviews. A place where they're safe, and no social media third party company can take them away. This works even better if you have your own driving instructors getting their reviews added to the website. How does any driving school get 'over 5000 five star reviews?' You're a driving school now and you need to think like a businessperson, a marketer, a salesperson.

Now when I say website, I'm not talking about one of these free hosted ones that look pretty but can't be found on Google by your potential customers. You need a professionally hosted website. Your website will need weekly if not daily attention. If you can't do this yourself, you'll need to pay someone to do it for you. You need to write articles, original articles, about all manner of things. The more content your website has, the more chance it has of being found. In the old days, to get a website found, the more links (backlinks) your website had, the higher in Google it went. Today Google and other search engines look for the content. It looks for 'are our customers (Google customers) going to find this useful?' I used to do our website but found it too time consuming. I knew how to do it, knew what articles to write but there were not enough hours in a day. I bit the bullet and employed someone fulltime. Having someone fulltime has meant our website has expanded 2650% in just over 2.5 years. Our graphics have improved and so much more.

Many people chose a website that they like the look of. It must be about your pupils and driving instructors. Some of the worst looking websites are the best performing. If you want to see an example of a website that is horrible but works incredibly well, google Ling car sales. This website is one of the best performing out there but has won awards for how ugly it is. If your website doesn't appear on at least page one of Google, it won't be found.

Let's revisit some of the different types of driving schools but from the school owner's perspective.

AN ADDITIONAL DRIVING INSTRUCTOR

You find yourself with too many pupils and think, I can get another driving instructor. You're probably busy because of recommendations or referrals. New pupils 'might' not be happy with somebody else besides you. When work dries up, can you still supply pupils? Often instructors in this situation, sell the extra pupils as referrals. If the other instructor does well, they get the credit but if it goes wrong, you get the flack. Will the new instructor teach like you do? Why are they short of work? Those are some of the questions you need to consider. This might seem like an easy way to start a driving school but you're probably building it with the wrong type of driving instructors.

A SMALL DRIVING SCHOOL

Starting this way gives you the opportunity to grow organically. Growing organically is to expand without raising a loan or ploughing money into your driving school. But and isn't there always a but, what comes first, the instructors or the work? Get the instructors first and you might not have pupils for them, get pupils first and you'll be disappointing pupils as you have no availability. A clear way to get a bad reputation! To be honest, we use a bit of both. If we have an area that we're turning away pupils in, we know we can add an instructor to the area. If we get an instructor first, we know we can use paid for advertising to get pupils. Luckily, experience has taught us how to write and set an advert so that we don't waste money.

One of the best ways to build your driving school is to train driving instructors yourself. This has a double win situation in that you can start to train driving instructors, not just in the DVSA qualifying tests but as instructors that will teach your way. What has been working for you, should work for other driving instructors who you train. One definition of a franchise I saw was 'a successful business model'. The idea is that if you follow someone who has done something that works, it must work for them too. Too many novice driving instructors don't copy a successful model and do their own thing. Facebook forums are full of these types, and I wince every time I see some of what's said. Remember, most driving instructors fail setting up their own school, if you're doing something different to the norm, you're more likely to succeed.

The successful driving schools won't shout from the rooftops what they do that works. Partly why I almost didn't write this chapter. I'm only going to show you some basic tricks, I save my real tricks for my own school. But it's not difficult to work out. Look at businesses outside of the driving world, and you can see how success can work.

There's no doubt in my mind, training my own instructors is the best way to grow your driving school but what about already qualified? I've spoken before of the pitfalls but what sort of qualified driving instructor would make a good fit for your school? I find success with driving instructors who've found the business side hard. They're a good instructor but, well poor businesspersons. They probably live in an area with fierce competition. This is no reflection on them but to compete with the big boys is hard. I know, my web positions almost always beat the 'big boys' website positions but it's a constant battle and daily work. To get a website in a good position is one battle, to keep it there is a lot more. I know they watch my site as I do theirs. There are many books written on website SEO and I've read a huge amount. Much of its trial and error and it changes all the time. You can't do all this AND be able to do driving lessons yourself. Don't kid yourself that you can. To build a good driving school, you're either going to have to learn yourself and become that person or continue doing driving lessons and pay someone. Oh, and beware, there are many people out there who will tell you they can get you to number one, few can. But get your website high and you'll capture a lot of pupils. The trick to any website is to give the customer what they want. Think about yourself. Let's say you want to buy a new television. You'll go on the internet to look at something you like, maybe even find the exact model. Then do a new search of that model to find the best price. Your search will start by looking for the features you want rather than the price. Most driving instructors think, pupils only want price but interestingly it's not all about price.

So what features are you going to sell for your driving school that attracts people to your school? One more tip on this before I move on. Your features must attract the sort of driving instructor you want. You're not looking for any instructor but the right driving instructors. Your features won't appeal to all driving instructors and that's okay, if they attract the right driving instructor.

SOCIAL MEDIA

You will need social media. Not just to attract pupils but social media is a great way to support your website. Note the wording, support your website. If you do posts of pupil passes, use links to your website. Link to specific pages. If a pupil passes a test in Budgie Town, link to the page for Budgie Town. If your page for Budgie Town driving lessons key word SEO's for 'driving lessons in Budgie Town', use this as the link to that page. There are more tricks to this as well but I'm just giving a few away remember. But the point is, make the post support the webpage. Send prospective pupils to your website from links. Write useful articles and link to them from social media. Remember, your website is here to stay, social media is there or not at the whim of a robot. That robot can decide to take you down and there's little you can do about it. You need to get as much traffic as possible going to the website. You can post special offers on social media that link to pages which aren't normally accessible from the website menu itself. These can be useful and make pupils feel special. But be very wary of any social media platform. I have seen many businesses run from social media only to have the whole lot shut down by the social media owners and there's nothing you can do about it. Social media supports your driving school, it doesn't run it.

Remember who your audience is too. I started my main Facebook page many years ago before I knew what I do now. I would, if starting again, restrict to pupils and potential pupils rather than lots of driving instructors. Just like everything, decide your message and think who your audience needs to be, then stick with it.

ADVERTISING

Running a driving school is going to mean advertising. I know there are many driving schools who say they don't need to do this but even if you're not advertising, you'll be marketing. Marketing your image to attract the best sort of pupils for your driving school and marketing to attract the right types of driving instructors for those pupils. By far the cheapest form of marketing is organic. This is when you don't have to pay for the advert, but pupils or instructors find you from search engines directly. Now when I say this is free, it isn't really, because to get this 'organic' marketing to work, takes time, skill, and money in the first place. Remember you have your two markets: pupils and instructors. I've found it best to separate the two websites, but others do it quite successfully with one website. Don't forget, most of my success came when I employed someone full time. I write the material while my marketing manager does the website magic. There are many different options that work but this is what has launched my business into overdrive.

In the meantime, there is 'paid for' advertising. Google, Bing, or Facebook all do paid ads. The beauty of these is, that you can turn them on or off to suit. These still require work though to work well. In the old days, Google would place the advert for position one depending on who bid the highest. Now Google looks at the customer experience, even in their adverts. 'Will your advert give their (Google) customers the best experience'. I'm afraid this comes down to not only the quality of the advert, but your website the advert links to again. It's a complicated algorithm only Google understands. But basically, you have a few words to bring your customers in. The first line is designed to make your reader read the second line, the second line to make them read the third line and the third line to make them click on the advert. It needs to speak to them. 'Would you like to know the secret of a good advert?' I bet you're saying yes! You would now read the next line and so on. 'I can show you in 3 easy steps!' And you're interested. There are many good books on how to write a good advert. I read lots of them but a particularly good one for me was 'How to write copy that sells' by Ray Edwards and I must recommend my friends book 'Big Ideas for small businesses' by John Lamerton. While I talk about Google, the same applies for Bing and to some degree, Facebook. Facebook is easier to target your adverts. The beauty with Facebook is, if you want to market to one handed jazz musicians living in Margate, you can. I have no idea if such an audience exists but if it does, Facebook will know. You can target and exclude markets as well. So, if you're looking for pupils, you say 'people with an interest in driving lessons' you can exclude 'driving instructors'. It's a shame most driving instructors don't know this as every day my feed is filled with driving lesson and related adverts. Heck, I'm not paying for that LOL.

Just like everything else, your advert needs to speak to the 'right' people. Especially when you are advertising for new instructors. Currently, my driving school could easily take on at least another 10 driving instructors. We turn so many pupils away, but this is the post COVID surge where every driving school is overrun with pupil enquires. Before COVID, we were turning away just 100 a week rather than a day so I base my potential on this as the bubble will burst soon. I predict around early 2024, we will see many instructors starting to struggle for work again from some driving schools. Schools will start to struggle as they haven't continued to market during this peak time. Peak because there are more pupils than ever looking at your website if you had one right now. More pupils than ever reading your message. More instructors than ever seeing what you do. Many have switched off everything and are sitting on their laurels. Keep focusing on marketing. Get your message right and the right people will come. The right people will make your business better and will improve things. The wrong ones will make your business hard and will destroy things. I cannot stress enough, think about who you want and actively look for them. Where would they be? What would they read? What would their hobbies be? Why do they want to join a driving school? Most of my market would probably not be on Facebook or would use it a lot. I have a few instructors that I think don't even know what Facebook LOL is.

Suffice to say, marketing and advertising are complex and took me a long time to learn. I attended many courses, joined business groups, and read a lot of material. As driving school owners, this is where your life changes too. If you'd rather keep doing the driving lessons, then you'll have to pay because all this stuff needs doing. It doesn't happen overnight.

Going hand in hand with the sort of driving instructor you want to attract and have work for you, you must look at your driving school image. Livery or not, website type and style. Company attire, vehicles, the whole lot needs to be considered. I started off not using full livery but using magnetic stickers for the cars and a roof box. Now I look after several driving schools and by far the most successful are the driving schools that use full livery. But I find it unpopular with some of the instructors. Now, when I interview potential driving instructors, I ask about their thoughts on livery, it's built into their contract too. Having livery, in my opinion, really starts to put your driving school on the map. There are huge advantages too. It's harder to damage the cars as those little supermarket door dings are harder to do to you. Pupils feel more confident when a liveried car pulls up outside their house too. The public start to notice the driving school more and enquiries come in. It's an odd phenomenon that when people see something several times, they start to trust it even though they may know nothing about the product. But above all for me, seeing my school with liveried cars was a proud moment. Even though I had been in business for 20 years, the livery felt like I had really got there. Currently I have a mix of livery and magnetics, but I want to go over to all liveried.

My livery matches my website and everything. Right down to the colours and the colours are complimented on something called a colour spectrum. Yeah, I had no idea either, but I know it works. The beauty of having a marketing manager with a degree in graphic design. We use the same on everything. Colour is very important too. Too many people chose a colour for their website or branding that they like, black, OMG black what is this saying to your customers. Yes, there is a complete science to this colour lark too. Blue gives the feeling of trust, green economy and so on. We have a mix of Blue and a ruddy maroon. This gives a warm trust feeling. Splashes of black, orange, and bright red yes, but not all over. Did you know that the best colour for putting the price of an offer in is orange? Yes, strange but it works. There are many books on this but 'Plan your website' by Steve Wood was a particularly good one for me.

Look outside of the driving school market for businesses that fit with your image. Are you a 'that'll do' sort of person or does it have to be exactly right? Fit the school and the image to the sort of person you are and attract similar people with your image.

While talking about image, I must mention again what you say. What you say in public and closed forums is important. Not least of all, the DVSA do monitor forums, open and closed. One wrong slip and it could come back to haunt you. Always act professional. I see far too many racist, bullying and just rude comments and it amazes me that these come from driving instructors. You want people to take you seriously and know you're professional. Keep an open mind to views posted.

I know today, some of the things I felt 20 years ago, I don't know. 20 years ago, if someone had said 'can they have the music on while on a lesson' I would have said no. Today, why not. Obviously, I would coach them into the advantages and disadvantages and what would they do if things got difficult. But my views changed on many things. As we mature as teachers, we learn different things and a good instructor will always be developing.

A MESSAGE FROM DAVE

I hope you find this book useful. While I have tried to cover everything, you need to know here, it is not exhaustive. This book is not only written to help you become a driving instructor, but to be a **good** driving instructor. I will always welcome suggestions for additions, so if you think I've missed anything, let me know.

As a driving instructor you have a choice. You can offer a mediocre service at best, cutting corners and following the 80% who are getting by or chose to be one of the 20% who take a great pride in what they do. Knowing you offer the best service; the correct knowledge and the best skill will make you a good driving instructor. It may sound like I've listed a lot of 'rules' here, but most of it is common sense and designed so we all sing from the same hymn sheet and work together. One thing I can tell you is that the business model is working. Just two years ago, my driving school was barely hitting 200 hits a month on the website, now its hitting over 5000. And it's only going up.

For many years I have campaigned for better standards in teaching. Often it can feel like you're hitting a brick wall when even some associations sacrifice standards for profit. So, I decided to improve standards with my own driving school. The instructors (that's you!) that we have now are brilliant and the best we've ever had. And the same goes for the promising and enthusiastic trainees we have coming through.

We're aiming for quality and not quantity in our team, something very few driving schools can say and something I am very proud to be building. I'd like to thank you all very much.

References

DVSA, n.d. *Approved driving instructor (ADI) register guide.* [Online]
Available at: https://www.gov.uk/government/publications/whats-involved-in-being-a-driving-instructor/approved-driving-instructor-adi-register-guide

Lamerton, J., 2019. In: *Routine Machine.* Plymouth: Tell your story, p. 276.

Wikipedia, n.d. *GROW medel.* [Online]
Available at: https://en.wikipedia.org/wiki/GROW_model
[Accessed 28 08 2021].

Appendixes
Appendix 1 the 17 standards

LESSON PLANNING

- Did the trainer identify the pupil's learning goals and needs?
- Was the agreed lesson structure appropriate for the pupil's experience and ability?
- Were the practice areas suitable?
- Was the lesson plan adapted, when appropriate, to help the pupil work towards their learning goals?

RISK MANAGEMENT

- Did the trainer ensure that the pupil fully understood how the responsibility for risk would be shared?
- Were directions and instructions given to the pupil clear and given in good time?
- Was the trainer aware of the surroundings and the pupil's actions?
- Was any verbal or physical intervention by the trainer timely and appropriate?
- Was sufficient feedback given to help the pupil understand any potential safety critical incidents?

TEACHING
& LEARNING
STRATEGIES

- Was the teaching style suited to the pupil's learning style and current ability?
- Was the pupil encouraged to analyse problems and take responsibility for their learning?
- Were opportunities and examples used to clarify learning outcomes?
- Was the technical information given comprehensive, appropriate, and accurate?
- Was the pupil given appropriate and timely feedback during the session?
- Were the pupils' queries followed up and answered?
- Did the trainer maintain an appropriate non-discriminatory manner throughout the session?
- At the end of the session – was the pupil encouraged to reflect on their own performance?

APPENDIX 2 DVSA CODE OF PRACTICE

The following extract is the DVSA's code of practice.

About the code

The Driver and Vehicle Standards Agency (DVSA) and the driver training industry place great emphasis on professional standards and business ethics.

This industry code of practice has been agreed between the National Associations Strategic Partnership (NASP) and DVSA.

It is a framework within which all instructors should operate. These professional bodies expect their members to adhere to this code of practice. The current NASP member groups are:

- Approved Driving Instructors National Joint Council (ADI NJC)
- Driving Instructors Association (DIA)
- The Motor Schools Association of Great Britain (MSA GB)

If you're an approved driving instructor (ADI) who agrees to follow the code, you can:

- Update your ADI registration to show you follow the code.
- Use the 'ADI code of practice - I've signed up' logo on your website or literature.

1. Personal conduct

Driver trainers will be professional, comply with the law, keep clients safe and treat them with respect.

The instructor agrees to:

- At all times behave in a professional manner towards clients in line with the standards in the national standard for driver and rider training
- At all times comply with legislative requirements including:
  - The protection of personal freedoms, the prevention of discrimination based on age, disability, gender, race, religion, or sexual orientation.
  - Not using mobile devices like phones when driving or supervising client's driving and only when parked in a safe and legal place.
  - Demonstrating a high standard of driving and instructional ability upholding safety standards including showing consideration for all other road users particularly pedestrians, cyclists, motorcyclists, and horse riders
  - Consumer, workplace and data protection regulations, the handling, storing, use and dissemination of video or audio recordings made in or around their tuition vehicle.
- Avoid inappropriate physical contact with clients.
- Avoid the use of inappropriate language to clients.
- Not initiate inappropriate discussions about their own personal relationships and take care to avoid becoming involved in a client's personal affairs or discussions about a client's personal relationships unless safeguarding concerns are raised.
- Avoid circumstances and situations which are or could be perceived to be of an inappropriate nature.
- Respect client confidentiality whilst understanding the actions to take if a client reveals concerns about

their private lives.

- Treat clients with respect and consideration and support them to achieve the learning outcomes in the national standard for driving cars and light vans (category B) as efficiently and effectively as possible
- Ensure that their knowledge and skills on all matters relating to the provision of driver training comply with current practice and legislative requirements.
- Use social network sites responsibly and professionally:
  - Ensuring that client's personal information is not compromised
  - Ensuring when using social media for marketing purposes that what is written is compliant with privacy and data protection legislation pertaining to digital communications, the laws regarding spam, copyright, and other online issues.
  - Treating other users of social media including clients, colleagues, and their views with respect
  - Be careful not to defame the reputation of colleagues, DVSA, driving examiners or the ADI register.
  - Not distribute, circulate, or publish footage taken of driving tests from in-car cameras, without permission from DVSA and the client

2. Business dealings

Driver trainers will account for monies paid to them, record client's progress, advise clients when to apply for their driving tests and guide them fairly through the learning process.

The instructor agrees to:

- Safeguard and account for any monies paid in advance by the client in respect of driving lessons, test fees or for any other purpose and make the details available to the client on request.

- On or before the first lesson make clients aware of both this code of practice and their terms of business which should include:
    - Legal identity of the school/instructor with full postal address and telephone number at which the instructor or their representative can be contacted.
    - The current price and duration of lessons
    - The current price and conditions for use of a driving school car for the practical driving test
    - The terms which apply to cancellation of lessons by either party
    - The terms under which a refund of lesson fees may be made.
    - The procedure for making a complaint.
- Check a client's entitlement to drive the vehicle and their ability to read a number plate at the statutory distance on the first lesson and regularly during their training.
- Make a record of a client's progress, which will include the number of lessons provided, and ensure that the client is aware of their progress and future training requirement to achieve their driving goals.
- Discuss with and advise a client when to apply for their driving tests, taking account of DVSA's cancellation rules, local waiting times and the instructor's forecast of a client's potential for achieving the driving test pass standard.
- Not cancel or rearrange a driving test without the client's knowledge and agreement, in the event of the instructor deciding to withhold the use of the school car for the driving test, sufficient notice should be given to the client to avoid loss of the DVSA test fee.
- Ensure that when presenting a client for the

practical driving test:

- The client has all the necessary documentation to enable the client to take the test.
- The vehicle complies with all aspects of motoring law, displays the instructor's certificate or licence correctly and is fitted with an extra interior rear-view mirror and correctly positioned L or optionally D plates in Wales.
- Accompany the client on their practical driving test and listen to the debrief, when requested to do so by the client.

3. Advertising

Driver trainers will take care to advertise and promote their businesses in a clear and fair manner.

The instructor agrees that:

- The advertising of driving tuition shall be clear, fair, and not misleading.
- Any claims made in advertising shall be capable of verification and comply with current CAP Advertising Codes
- Advertising that refers to pass rates should not be open to misinterpretation and the basis on which the calculation is prepared should be made clear.

4. Conciliation

Driver trainers will deal promptly with any complaints received and aim for speedy resolution of any grievances.

The instructor agrees that:

- Complaints by clients should be made in the first instance to the driving instructor, driving school or contractor following the training provider's complaints procedure.
- If, having completed the procedure, the client has been unable to reach an agreement or settle a dispute further guidance may be sought:

- If a client believes that their instructor is not providing a satisfactory business service they can contact their local Citizens Advice Bureau for guidance
- If clients are unhappy with their instructor's professional service, the client can contact the ADI Registrar by emailing instructorconduct@dvsa.gov.uk

———

[1]

Printed in Great Britain
by Amazon

38228060R00205